WHERE SPIRITUALITY & JUSTICE MEET

Spiritual Formation & Integral Mission

WHERE SPIRITUALITY & JUSTICE MEET

Spiritual Formation & Integral Mission

EDITED BY STEVE BRADBURY & LYN JACKSON

GRACEW♦RKS
Truth for Life
www.graceworks.com.sg

Published by Melbourne School of Theology
5 Burwood Highway,
Wantirna VIictoria 3152
Australia
Tel: +613 9881 7800
Email: mst@mst.edu.au
Website: www.mst.edu.au

Co-published by Graceworks Private Limited
22 Sin Ming Lane
#04–76 Midview City
Singapore 573969
Tel: 67523403
Email: enquiries@graceworks.com.sg
Website: www.graceworks.com.sg

Cover Photo by Phil Sparrow

ISBN: 978-981-11-6662-4

1 2 3 4 5 6 7 8 9 10 • 25 24 23 22 21 20 19 18

CONTENTS

Contributors v

Introduction xi
Steve Bradbury

Intentional Spiritual Growth in Incarnational Ministry 1
Ruth Bryce

"Being" and "Doing" in an Unjust World 23
Lee Chee Loi

Yelling at God About Poverty 43
Clint Bergsma

Spiritual Formation, Leadership & Kingdom Ministry 65
Margaret Loy Choon Ming

Contemplation and Action:
An exploration of a symbiotic relationship............................ 87
Lee Soo Choo

Living and Leading in Spirit and Truth 105
Steve Gumaer

The Screwtape Blog 119
Lyn Jackson

The Ripple Effect:
The power of worldview to subjugate spiritual formation in regard
to gender-based violence 143
Rosemary Hack

Lessons in Faith from the Karen People of Myanmar 163
Oddny Gumaer

Contributors

STEVE BRADBURY is the course coordinator for Eastern College Australia's Master of Transformational Development. Prior to joining Eastern's faculty in 2009, he served as the national director of TEAR Australia (1984–2009), the inaugural chair of Micah Global (1999–2009), the inaugural co-chair and subsequently the chair of the International Board of Micah Challenge (2003–4, 2008–12).

RUTH BRYCE is a speech therapist turned development worker who has been living with her family in Cambodia since 2006. Serving cross culturally with Interserve, she is passionate about justice, knowing people and being known, and joining God in what He is doing in the place her family calls home.

LEE CHEE LOI serves on the board of Malaysian Care, a leading Christian development and social service organisation in Malaysia, where he was executive director for 13 years until his retirement in 2011. He also provides strategic advisory help to Dignity for Children Foundation, another Malaysian NGO. Prior to this, he worked in the human resource industry at the senior management level in major corporations.

CLINTON BERGSMA manages international partner relations for Amos Australia. He enjoys considering the practical implications of the kingdom of God and exploring the undeclared theologies that underpin the way we live and act.

MARGARET LOY CHOON MING is the executive director of Community Transformation Initiative, a non-profit entity for the alleviation of poverty and the promotion of human flourishing among the vulnerable people in Malaysia. She is passionate about helping the church and Christians understand their wider responsibility to society and the world, and assisting them as they seek to express God's love in practical and culturally relevant ways. She is a former advocate and solicitor and a youth pastor who finds joy bringing her experience of both together in her work and ministry.

LEE SOO CHOO is currently program manager at Community Transformation Initiative, a small non-profit in Kuala Lumpur, Malaysia. After learning to walk with "two feet of love" in Malaysia and Afghanistan, she continues to strive to be at the place where her deep gladness and the world's deep hunger meet.

STEVE GUMAER is the co-founder and president of Partners Relief & Development, an organization that has been working in places where violence and political complexity prevent children from thriving, for the past 25 years. He and his wife Oddny run the organization from Norway along with three daughters and a dog named Floyd. He loves to rock climb and sit by a campfire with good friends after a day in the wilderness.

LYN JACKSON loves to tell stories about the creativity and resilience of ordinary people trapped in poverty, and about the God who expresses His care for them through His people. She has worked as an educator and communications professional in Christian development agencies in India, Nepal, and Australia; seeking to encourage Christians to be part of God's global mission of compassion and justice.

Rosemary Hack is the director of AIDSLink International. She is passionate about tackling issues of injustice and oppression, and believes that disrupting the theology and beliefs that lie below the surface is a key part of this.

Oddny Gumaer is the co-founder of Partners Relief & Development. She has spent more than 20 years working with refugees and internally displaced peoples in Myanmar and the Middle East. She loves being a part of transforming lives and bringing about change in communities. She currently lives in Norway with her family.

INTRODUCTION

Steve Bradbury

Many a time during my 25 years working with TEAR Australia (a faith-based aid and development organisation) people would ask me, "Given all the time you spend visiting communities suffering great hardships, why aren't you depressed, or disenchanted, or angry, or cynical, or...?"

Of course, there were times of deep sadness. Sitting on a bookshelf in my study is a lovely photo of three young South African girls. It is getting old now, slowly turning sepia. But Sindiwe, the beautiful, effervescent girl in the centre of the photo, never had the chance to grow old. A few months after I met her in Tennyson House, a shelter for homeless girls in Durban, she was reunited with her grandmother, a cause for much rejoicing. But a short time later, she died in the inferno caused by the firebombing of her grandmother's tiny wooden home—a tragic death caused by a rent dispute. I wept when I heard the news.

Even now, nearly 20 years later, when I sit with the photo as I did a few days ago, I am filled with sadness. I keep the photo to remind me of the terrible circumstances in which so many people are forced to live and die. But neither sadness nor anger dominated my feelings during the many occasions I had the privilege of spending time in extremely disadvantaged and marginalised communities.

There is a simple reason for this: whenever I went into such communities, there was always someone holding my hand, often literally. That someone was a person quietly immersed in doing the work of compassion and justice, doing so out of friendship with Jesus, and love for neighbour. Being in their presence, walking with them in their context, albeit briefly, was to be granted a special taste of the kingdom of God. What lies at the heart of this Kingdom is hope and love, not despair.

These beautiful colleagues, of course, experience times of soul-wrenching distress, times when a cry of anguish is the only legitimate response. And the Jesus who stood outside the tomb of his friend expressed precisely such pain. His was a cry of deep grief and equally deep love. But also anger—anger at that which was profoundly wrong. This was not how things were supposed to be. So he acted. Jesus was neither immune to grief nor captive to it.

Where did Jesus find the strength to continue? And how do those called to serve the economically poor—people almost always pushed to the margins of society and often systematically exploited by those with influence and power—find the strength? This second question is the focus of this book.

Many helpful books have been written about spiritual formation, and at least some of them are by authors who recognise the need to integrate faith and service to the poor. But it would not surprise me if this collection of essays were unique, because each of these authors is a transformational development practitioner.

The essays were originally written as part of their Master of Transformational Development (MTD) studies,[1] but far more important than that, each author knows from personal experience that our ongoing

---

[1] See Master of Transformational Development. N.d. Retrieved March 1, 2018 (https://www. eastern.edu.au/courses/master-transformational-development).

capacity to "do justice and love mercy and walk humbly with God"[2] requires a God-nurtured resilience.

Jeffrey P. Greenman offers the following definition of spiritual formation:

> Spiritual formation is our continuing response to the reality of God's grace shaping us into the likeness of Jesus Christ, through the work of the Holy Spirit, in the community of faith, *for the sake of the world* (my emphasis).[3]

As the one given the honour of facilitating the MTD programme, I get to ask a lot of questions! With respect to the definition above, I asked: How do we cooperate with this work of grace, and what practices and habits may help us in this ongoing process of transformation? What has been your experience of the different spiritual disciplines in the nurturing of your faith and discipleship? What role can local communities of faith or Christian development NGOs play in enhancing the spiritual formation of members and staff? What role have they played in your life and work?

It was wrestling with such questions and others like them that emerged out of the students' own experience, that resulted in the content of this book. I trust that you will learn as much as I did when I first read these essays, and that you will be as encouraged, challenged, and moved as I was.

Steve Bradbury
Co-ordinator, Master of Transformational Development
Director, Micah 6:8 Centre
Eastern College Australia

---

[2] Mic. 6:8. See also Matt. 23:23.
[3] Greenman, Jeffrey P. 2010. "Spiritual Formation in Theological Perspective." Pp. 23–35 in *Life in the Spirit: Spiritual Formation in Theological Perspective,* edited by Jeffrey P. Greenman and George Kalantzis. Downers Grove, IL: InterVarsity Press.

INTENTIONAL SPIRITUAL GROWTH IN INCARNATIONAL MINISTRY

Ruth Bryce

How does the experience of living cross-culturally in incarnational ministries in poor communities nurture our development as Jesus-following counter-cultural people?

Making a commitment to follow Jesus involves a lifetime of having our identity and character shaped, as well as growing in our understanding of God Himself. As Christians, we are invited to be transformed by the renewing of our mind and to embrace the abundant life which Jesus came to give (Rom. 8:29; John 10:10). Willard describes this process as being "inwardly transformed in such a way that the personality and deeds of Jesus Christ naturally flow out from them when and wherever they are" (Willard, n.d.:5). Seeking to live a gospel-orientated life is a counter-cultural experience, no matter where we are situated. Matthew's record of Jesus' "Sermon on the Mount" provides many practical implications of the counter-cultural values on which God's kingdom is based (Matt. 5). Averbeck (2008) asserts that while the Old Testament role of the prophet was specific to a few, the salvation Jesus offers widens this prophetic role to *all* Christians. All Christians are called to live lives that are distinct from their surrounding culture, so that others may see God's glory. The defining distinctive is love.

Spiritual growth requires both an act of God's spirit and a persons willingness to learn and be shaped by Him. Cross-cultural experience is not a superior means of attaining this, or even a guarantee that spiritual growth occurs. However, for many who intentionally seek to know God more, being outside their own culture has an intensifying effect on their spiritual growth. This paper draws on writings on spiritual growth, reflections from cross-cultural workers, personal communication, and my own experience. The majority of voices in this paper come from those who have been involved in incarnational ministry for more than eight years, so while including many examples of difficulty, their reflections focus on what has helped them sustain this lifestyle over the longer term.

INCARNATIONAL CROSS-CULTURAL WORKERS

This paper is particularly interested in the spiritual growth of those involved in what is broadly known as 'incarnational ministry'. Typically, organisations and movements who use 'incarnational' language to describe their mission point to Jesus coming from heaven, becoming a man and living amongst the people to whom he came to reveal God. Jesus did not come in power and glory. He deliberately came in weakness and vulnerability; lived in a common home; and chose an outcast, lowly status for himself and well-known sinners to be amongst his disciples. However, through his death, Jesus ushered in a powerful new age of love and redemption available for all humanity.

Viewing Jesus' words as instructive—"As you have sent me into the world, so I have sent them into the world" (John 17:18; ESV)—these organisations seek to enter communities, not in the powerful position of an outside expert, but in a learning posture which seeks to "share their lives with the urban poor and live out the Gospel among their neighbours" (Servant Partners, 2017).

Incarnational ministry is often promoted as a missional strategy—to come amongst those living in slums and share the good news of Jesus through experiencing life together. However, most incarnational workers see their relocation to poor communities as a prophetic act of obedience to God, dramatically rejecting the global trends of materialism and consumerism and orientating their life to kingdom values.

Bessenecker explains that incarnational mission aims to see communities transformed through offering an alternative story to the "meritocracy, resignation, cynicism, naiveté and complacency... (of) the destructive worldviews, social patterns and cultural narrative from which our globe suffers" (2010:60). Essentially, it echoes the calling of all followers of Jesus, to bear witness to him in living out the values of the kingdom, which he summed up in his two commandments: "Love God and love our neighbour as ourselves" (Matt. 22:37–40; ESV).

Foster describes an incarnational approach as "sacramental living... to do our work as Jesus would work if he were in our place" (2004:217). He affirms this as bringing religious life into everyday life, so that daily decisions, interactions, purpose and ministry give glory to God, because "people desperately need to see the reality of God made visible and manifest" (Foster, 2004:219).

Foster points to Dag Hammarskjöld, former Secretary-General of the United Nations, as someone "who embraced devotion and work as a seamless garment", a characteristic Foster regards as essential in the incarnational tradition (2004:215). Interestingly, Hammarskjöld lived far from the slums of the majority world, illustrating that cross-cultural ministry among the poor is only one aspect of incarnational ministry. Thus, a defining characteristic of incarnational approach is living an integrated life, "keeping Jesus as our ever-present teacher" (Foster, 2004:220).

CULTURE

In any discussion on cross-cultural living, it is important to define culture. Lingenfelter and Mayers refer to culture as the "point of reference by which people comprehend themselves and others" (1986:122). While culture is related to nationhood, religion, and generational norms; it is not defined by them, as each group will have subgroups where their experience, traditions and beliefs hold them apart from others in the larger collective.

> Culture is not something you can measure.... However, like an onion, you can "peel" culture and strip down its layers. The outermost layer... is what you can see, hear, and touch: artifacts, products, and rituals. The next layer of a culture consists of its systems and institutions. Systems and institutions, in turn, are based on certain beliefs, norms, and attitudes. These beliefs then stem from the core of the "onion", the most basic values of any culture. (InterNations, 2015)

The onion analogy is useful as it helps to explain why changing clothing and participating in rituals do not mark a deep cultural change. It also allows for the experience some people living cross-culturally describe as 'culture stripping', "the slow peeling back of layers and layers of self—it's painful but it's good pain" (Pieh-Jones, 2013). The "good" aspect to the pain that Pieh-Jones alludes to is the self-revelatory process of understanding ourselves better. Although it is painful, as we surrender what we find to the Father, who both created us and loves us, this can be catalytic for ongoing spiritual growth.

IDENTITY

Culture is closely linked to identity. Therefore, as we live immersed in another culture for the long term, it is not only our practice that changes; our identity is also influenced. Across different seasons of ministry, the level of importance cross-cultural workers place on their nationality fluctuates.

In my own experience, the first season of ministry was about investing our lives in a Cambodian poor urban community. We modified our lives so we lived in a similar house, ate similar food, and had similar rhythms and routines (apart from our weekly breaks outside). In many ways, we minimised our Australian-ness. Frustratingly, though, the community identified us by our foreignness. It was a significant victory when I started being referred to as "mother of Abby" rather than "the foreign lady".

Nine years on, I am more comfortable with the title of "the foreign lady"; it is an obvious way to describe me! I have made peace with this, confronting some of the pride that pushed me to reject it. Whilst I still desire to be seen as someone who knows and understands my context and community, I am content with the realisation that as an "inside-outsider", God has been able to use me to affirm and encourage kingdom values in local Christians, who find themselves at odds with local culture because of their faith in Jesus.

Greenfield also recounts this prophetic role: "Paradoxically for me, who sought to become an insider, one of the most significant roles I have played in the slum and in the Asian church is that of a stranger, a prophet who comes with an outsider's alternative perspective" (Bessenecker, 2010:47).

A key stressor of cross-cultural life is dealing with ambiguity. There is an ongoing sense of not quite understanding the story we have just entered, but also ambiguity in finding our place within this new world. Cross-cultural living thrusts us into the midst of many cultures. Jones (2015) points out that mission life brings you into a plethora of different subcultures, and many are different from the anticipated culture you came to serve. For example, across my week, I work amongst multinational teams, enter the international school community, engage in the local Christian community, and live within the poor urban community. Each of these communities has its own culture, even though geographical proximity is high. Involvement in each of these stretches a person in new and different ways.

One of my high stressors during the early years was negotiating the frequent transitions between these different cultures, which often felt like moving between worlds (particularly expatriate and urban poor) within the same location. Within this daily transition, the complexity of our idealised identity (identifying and living in solidarity with the poor) made painful collisions with my seemly contradictory actual living self (still enjoying peaceful café getaways away from the slums and Cambodian culture). I relate to Nouwen's assurance that growing in our identity in Christ as "Christ's beloved" is surely an anchor which holds us fast through both superficial and deeper identity questions (1992).

A common theme amongst incarnational workers is their own brokenness and limitations, and being confronted with the surfacing of undesirable values and attitudes.

> I have cussed more, cried more, been more angry, had less faith, been more cynical and... have become in many ways a worse person during my last two years of serving in Asia. (Parker, 2012)

Many incarnational workers tell stories of the devastating discovery that the honourable desires they demonstrated to the world in moving to the slums were not so pure. Hidden not far under the surface lies what Richard Rohr (1989) describes as the "shadow side" of our personality, polluting our motivation. Much of this awareness comes directly from being amongst another culture. "Most missionaries who become genuinely incarnated in another culture experience a heightened sense of moral and ethical responsibility. They become aware of areas of sin in their lives to which they had previously become blinded by their own culture" (Lingenfelter and Mayers, 1986:122). As this is revealed, we can choose to conceal this aspect of who we are, or turn towards it, work on it together with God, and reduce the power it has in our lives. Surely the latter is an example of the character refinement that Willard calls "renovation of the heart" (2002).

Longer-term cross-cultural living also brings opportunity to address false identities and idols. Pieh-Jones (2013) reminds us that the very identity of being a culturally sensitive, acclimatised, linguistically fluent missionary can become an unhealthy idol. Duncan (2005:8) shares his profound disappointment and underlying hurt to his pride following returning from incarnational ministry in Manila, revealing the idolatry that becoming a missionary had become.

As well as the 'super missionary' complex, incarnational workers can also fall prey to the 'messiah complex', when our view of the needs around us distorts our idea of what is required to save people. We forget that it is *Jesus* they need, rather than us. In his teaching about healthy teams, Jack encouraged cross-cultural workers to attend to their spiritual life and practice spiritual disciplines as an antidote to this. Barker speaks of the importance of finding our own place in the team and ministry, and not being restricted by the example of people we look up to (2003:32). Honesty and humility before God involve discovering who He has made us to be, not putting on the mask of others. Cross-cultural living can help self-discovery and acceptance as God's child. Manning writes: "When I get honest, I admit that I am a bundle of paradoxes... To live by grace means to acknowledge my whole life's story, the light side and the dark" (1990).

Trotter helpfully explores this idea of living with ambiguity, and holding the contradictions and limitations that we bring. She encourages her readers to embrace the 'and's in life, rather than living lives which are based on an 'either-or' paradigm (Trotter, 2015). Likewise, Foster urges us to draw near to God's grace: "This side of eternity we will never unravel the good from the bad, the pure from the impure. But what I have come to see is that our God is big enough to receive us with all the mixture. We do not have to be bright or pure or filled with faith" (1981:78).

An opportunity exists, then, to view one's own culture and values from the perspective of an outsider. Brant helpfully uses the image of changing the spectacles you wear to illustrate how familiarity with more than one culture influences our perception of faith and culture.

> What I learned... is that some people have mistaken the Good News to be changing... spectacles for new ones. We have reduced the Gospel to be an exchange of values and habits.... [I]n both cultures I reside in... there are good values and bad values... we are differently good and differently bad. We are quite equally flawed, not one culture can claim superiority to teach the other much... there is more than one right way to be Christian. When

you see Jesus differently, your walk with Jesus is going to look differently. (Brant, 2015)

Brant posits that spectacles from any one culture will only allow us to see certain aspects of the God we love, but not the whole kingdom of God. This partial revelation echoes 1 Corinthians 13:12: "For now we see only a reflection as in a mirror. Then shall we see face to face. Now I know in part; then shall I know fully, even as I am fully known." The cross-cultural worker has the opportunity to appreciate diversity as authored by God, "for all the less than appealing features of cultural and ethnic variety, important insights about God and his world go undiscovered if we avoid creative engagement with human diversity" (Elmer, 1993:23).

The apostle Paul's imagery of us holding treasure in earthen vessels (2 Cor. 4) is a useful analogy as we consider the inherent bias and weakness of any given culture. Seeing our flawed yet partly redeemed cultures as vessels helps us be confident to experience God through different traditions, where "we worship God not the form" (Foster, 2004:217). This requires a humble acceptance that we may not yet know all there is to know of 'kingdom culture'. This awareness appears yo be a useful platform for spiritual growth, as it helps bring us into the posture of a life-long learner.

Lingenfelter and Mayers see opportunity in cross-cultural living for becoming more like Christ, especially in regard to what Paul described as "becoming all things to all men" (1 Cor. 9; NASB). Cross-cultural workers often have some of their Christian identity stripped away. 'Markers' that distinguished them as a Christian in their home country may not be available or seen as culturally appropriate in their new context.

For some people, attending a church is not possible, or services may be so different they do not fulfil any of the needs that going to church did at home. For people who are used to sharing their faith eloquently, language learning reduces one's expression level to that of a child, rendering the speaker helpless to clarify their motivations (Barker, 2003:44). In cultures where local practice is often at odds with Christian understanding (for example, men frequenting prostitutes and viewing pornography; women gambling together socially), tensions arise between relationship-building and personal integrity.

Ambiguity abounds as indirect communication styles, and limited language and understanding of cultural cues and traditions bring about situations that are confusing. For a while at least, the worker's identity as 'salt and light' appears threatened. Their distinctiveness is attributed to their foreignness, not to their faith.

I still remember my joy and relief when, after six months of living in the community, one of my neighbours shared her question about why, as an obviously rich family, we allowed our children to play with other children in the community. "All the children, not just the ones from good families.... (You) allowed Vietnamese children to play too. This was very different to Khmer families—they did not allow this". It was one of those beautiful moments when I could share, with this lady who lived in the dirt floor squatter shack across the lane, how I followed Jesus and He taught that all people had value to Him, especially children.

Eight years later, I had the privilege of being with this same lady as her baby boy died from a liver condition. In the preceding weeks, she had, with confidence, dedicated him to Jesus, and today speaks of her son living in Jesus' house, healthy and with lots of food to eat. To be honest, at the time she was commenting on our inclusive policy for child play, I had no idea which children were Vietnamese and which were Khmer, but the conversation was significant for me as a timely reminder of God's faithfulness and sovereignty in being able to take the clumsy attempts we make at showing love, and use them to touch the hearts of others. Seeking to find God speaking and acting in the everyday has grown my trust in God, and hopefully brings openness to his Spirit's prompting.

SUFFERING

As incarnational workers embed their own lives amongst people whose lives are ensnared in complex social, economic, and physical circumstances, they are confronted by some of the pain and suffering their neighbours experience. In personal interviews about spiritual practices, an experienced missionary describes her practice of bi-monthly fasting to combat the spiritual darkness encountered by those she works with: "We realised early on that there was not a lot that we could actually do to help people; much of what people were working through were issues that God would continue to heal and refine over their lifetime" (Bryce, Cheng, and Gumear, 2015).

Matheson states: "When we pray with another person we are... saying that the difficulty is beyond our capacity... and that relief will come only if God intervenes" (2010:138). Powerlessness to improve circumstances and events can be very confronting. Workers often find themselves worn out by the ever-changing crises and continual needs which surround them. Haynes explains: "There is a random dynamic that goes with living in incarnational community in the slums... needs often catch us unprepared and are tailgated rapidly by others" (Bessenecker, 2010:139).

Barker (2003) shares details of crying out to God as his family listened to violence happening across the street. They felt powerless to help, paralysed by cultural complexities that meant that immediate intervention would bring greater shame and more violence the next day. Aside from family conflict; systemic evil including child trafficking, drug manufacturing, and mafia-style control are also often present in communities where incarnational workers seek to live and minister.

Prince shares how these experiences can lead to changes in how workers relate to God: "After a significant time among our friends in poverty, many of the prayers we used to pray, the worship songs we used to sing and the devotional readings we used to partake in no longer seem relevant" (Bessenecker, 2010:106). It can be at the very point of reaching the end of ourselves that God invites us to a deeper experience of him. Prince and Heuertz declare: "We crave a deeper well to quench the thirst of our soul and that of our neighbours" (Bessenecker, 2010:106). Viewing rhythms of rest and retreat as essential for their own longevity, Teague links this surrendering to God, as growing our trust: "Many situations—especially the worst—cannot be controlled. Or solved. Or helped. They just are and they require us just to be. In that being—in our relationship with the person we are serving—we have to trust the presence of Christ to minister through us" (2012:126).

Duncan (2006) and Toan (2012) both see a strong 'theology of suffering' as essential for longevity for incarnational workers. Duncan warns that without this, workers leave disillusioned and burnt out. Porterfield affirms this: "If we pick up our cross and follow Jesus on this narrow path of radical, wholistic love, we will have trials and suffering." He goes on the explain that those who have a biblical theology of suffering are better equipped to "see how God's sovereign plan can even use the suffering of His saints to further His Kingdom and His renown" (Porterfield, 2006).

A static theology, developed prior to entry into the cross-cultural context, will be insufficient for the long-term. New cultural lenses, new levels of suffering, new revelations of personal frailness—all need to be integrated into our understanding of the gospel.

Jack explains how Servant teams seek to support each other in their struggles and allow hard questions: "When faced with poverty, suffering and evil, we sometimes find ourselves forced to rethink our faith in new ways... we want our community to be a safe place" (Servants to Asia's Urban Poor, 2013).

TEAM AND COMMUNITY

In researching spiritual practices of incarnational workers, Toan (2012) noted: "Responders valued their communities as helping to maintain spiritual practices, giving space for accountability, engendering encouragement, understanding the hardships and giving support". Smith agrees: "Community is vitally important for sustainability in incarnational ministry... they need faithful brothers and sisters who will walk beside them in the pilgrimage" (Bessenecker, 2012:14). Living and working in a healthy community not only supports workers, but it is also a prophetic manifestation of the kingdom of God. Trotter (2013) recommends community life to cross-cultural workers to maintain a connection with the broader body of Christ:

We may lead very different-looking lives, but we bear the same image of God. We may shoulder different responsibilities, but we share the same human need for unconditional love and acceptance... I believe he (God) wants all of us to experience authentic, life-giving community.

Duncan describes his experience of a team:

Most of our team meetings were reduced to tearful sessions; a chance to cry and not be ashamed. Through our tears we saw all that was not needed in our lives. Somehow our tears had a healthy dismantling effect. It was as though God was wiping our eyes, to see who we really were and who we needed to become. (2007:28)

My own experience of weekly 'team times' nurtured my intimacy with Jesus through expressions of worship, prayer and spending time together. Belonging to a community where we regularly share deeply allowed me to be carried in times of deep stress, as well as support others in their time of disillusionment or exhaustion. The level of accountability and vulnerable sharing was far beyond any church community or workplace we had been part of in an Australian context. I regarded my weekly team sharing times as part of my rhythms of spiritual practice.

Toan's research, however, hinted at the shadow side of community, with more than half of the participants listing team life as a stressor in their life (2012). Haynes admits: "Most people come to community with higher expectations for it than aptitude to express it" (Bessenecker, 2010:48). My own team experience has included unhealthy comparisons with other workers, individualism and pride as potential traps of community life. Barker reminds us that "how we deal with... (another's) imperfection is a sign of our maturity as people" (2003:33). Community life provides opportunities for our character to be revealed. For a community to be a place of trust, it needs to be marked by God's forgiveness and grace.

As part of our team covenant, two of the items we commit to are

"Praying for each other and seeking each other to grow in relationship with God and general wellbeing" and "Establishing our own rhythms which are healthy and sustainable... as well as shared rhythms of rest..." These points hold in tension the interdependence which team life requires, prayer, and service towards one another and taking responsibility for one's own spiritual growth. Negotiating this in a healthy manner requires ongoing intentionality, grace, and the activity of God's Spirit in each of our lives.

SPIRITUAL PRACTICES

Incarnational living can also change some of the spiritual practices that we previously used in relating to God. For me, things like not having access to worship music were difficult. Living simply 'like our neighbours' meant limited technology in a time when computers and smartphones were not yet popular in Cambodia. It became an important aspect of our Sabbath rest day (spent out of community) to have worship music playing in the background.

Making our homes in new places involves creatively maintaining some of the familiar routines that sustain us, as well as adopting new ones. I have found the beauty of a sunset viewed across the rusty roof while preparing our evening meal, to be a moment of God's grace in the midst of both the poverty outside and the family responsibilities inside.

As cross-cultural workers seek to identify with their neighbours, people frequently encounter a new level of suffering. Amongst those who stay in their new culture longer term, Pieh-Jones (2013) describes an aspect of identity adjustment as "culture pain". She explains this as different from earlier culture shock:

> Culture pain comes when the difficult... confusing aspects of a new culture begin to affect you at a deep, personal level.... Things like corruption and poor health care, attitudes toward HIV, education of girls, adoption, or poverty, religious rituals, children's rites of passage, are not theoretical anymore.... These issues are now yours to navigate. And sometimes, that hurts.

A reality of living in the midst of a poor community is that our communities contain dark places, where horrible things happen, often. Evil and darkness exist here in a way that few have experienced in 'regular life' in the west. In a caution to people who refute the existence of evil, Barker declares: "Evil is well-organised, shifty and personal, affecting everyone in the world" (2003:168).

Duncan calls Christians to acknowledge the spiritual battle which they engage: "The saddest truth on the planet is that few Christians spend intimate quality time with the one they have made their deepest promises too... relating to God on the run... hardly conducive to prepare us for life in a war zone" (2005:50).

Prayer

Toan (2012) found that prayer was the "most important factor in sustaining spiritual life". People cited pursuing refreshment through prayer groups, prayer spaces, centring prayer, contemplative prayer, the practice of examen, and finding spaces outside of the local community.

Matheson (2010) speaks of his own prayer life being renewed through his contact with the suffering of the poor around him (2010:139). Barker shares:

> My contemplation can be overwhelming as reality sobers me out of my pettiness... I have faith however that because I keep putting myself in a receptive space the connections will come regardless of how I feel at a given time... traditionally the scriptures, spiritual guides and solitude have been the ways to put up our antennae to catch the longing of God. (2003:35)

Heuertz and Prince tell of their inner-change experience:

> Because the need for transformation in our neighbourhoods is so great, we press into intimacy with Jesus through individual and collective rhythms of prayer, Sabbath silence and solitude.

Without the riches delved in contemplation, we have nothing to give. (Bessenecker, 2010:107)

Barker, in critiquing potential cross-cultural workers, cites a strong devotional life as an essential quality, for the purposes of being "able to fan into flame the spark that was placed in them" (2003:127).

Growth and maturity in cross-cultural ministry are needed to retain our "sense of dependence on and unwavering trust in God and his word" (Lingenfelter and Mayers, 1986:123). Toan insists a well-developed theology is important for both resilience and discernment "as we walk the unknown path" (2012).

We must acknowledge how easily we are deceived... by our sinful selves and the sin of our culture. It's true, we are shaped by what we're saturated in, which is why incarnation must always be paired with devotion. (Prince and Heuertz, in Bessenecker, 2010:105)

The themes of trust, surrender, and submission to God reoccur within these writings. In my experience, these are acts that are repeated throughout our lives and sometimes throughout the day. Incarnational living provides many new circumstances to trust God in, especially as He peels back the layers of our deeper beliefs which direct our behaviour and attitudes. As workers, we need to trust God to hold us through these times of uncertainty and give us what we need when we need it. It comes down to trust, knowing that we are held by God. Lingenfelter and Mayer helpfully remind us:

We must begin the incarnational process by accepting... [that] God has made us and that what He has done is good... If we do not accept the goodness of His past work in our lives, we will likely not to trust His future working in us. (1986:121)

Interestingly, Lingenfelter sees the effect of not being able to do this as detrimental, not just to ourselves, but also to cross-cultural work, as "we will never be able to accept his (God's) work in the lives of others who are culturally different from us" (1986:122).

RHYTHMS OF REST AND SABBATH

Many incarnational workers identify strongly as activists, yet many who endure long term have strict rhythms around rest, contemplation, and setting aside time with God. Mother Teresa describes her own experience:

> We need to find God, and he cannot be found in the noise and restlessness. God is the friend of silence. See how nature—trees, flowers, grass—grows in silence; see the stars, the moon and the sun, how they move in silence... we need silence to be able to touch souls. (1985:107)

Pausing and spending time with God is not just about refreshing and re-energising to continue to do the same thing for a longer duration. It is expecting that we ourselves are changed, moved, and helped to discern through spending time in the presence of God. As Prince says, contemplation "sustains our member's sacrificial living... but also matters because our contemplative engagement can be good news for our neighbours" (Bessenecker, 2010:109).

Willard reminds us of the essentialness of communing with God, lamenting that "we have omitted the making of disciples and neglected to enroll Christ's workers as Christ's students... as a result the non-disciple has something more important to do than to become like Jesus" (Shaw, 2014). Shaw also warns that Christians are rarely taught how to thrive and be healthy 'message bearers' who "diligently develop inner life", and see growth in their spiritual qualities (2015:2).

BARRIERS TO SPIRITUAL GROWTH

Throughout the writings of incarnational workers, there is an acknowledgement that these spiritual disciplines, which we know are so important, are often difficult for workers to commit to and sustain. One of the challenges identified is that incarnational life often has a sense of immediacy, and daily life events involve flexibility on a daily basis. Within my family, Cambodia is affectionately known as "the land of Plans A, B, C and D, and that's just before lunch". Keeping disciplines in the face of community hospitality, let alone community crisis, is often just not possible.

C. S. Lewis gently encourages us that perhaps it is indeed our perspective that is in need of changing, rather than the circumstances:

> The great thing, if one can, is to stop regarding all the unpleasant things as interruptions of ones 'own' or 'real' life. The truth is of course that what one calls the interruptions are precisely one's real life... what one calls one's real life is a phantom of one's own imagination. (Foster, 2004)

Prince, however, rejects the excuses of chickens, children, downstairs karaoke and other issues of exterior context as the true reasons for people not following spiritual disciplines. Instead, he names our 'interior' as presenting the greatest obstacle.

> Contemplative intimacy with our God is completely countercultural and counter to our sinful nature as humans—it dismantles our personal, cultural, and religious illusions... that is excruciatingly difficult for us... so we resist. (Bessenecker, 2010:119)

Taylor, too, points out that prayer does not come naturally and it is especially a problem for minds influenced by scientific empiricism to believe in a God who answers prayers (1972:223). His advice in these circumstances is to reaffirm that God is beyond our understanding, both accepting the reality of God and letting Him be God, rather than having Him live by the rules that we construct for Him.

CONCLUSION

A developed spiritual life comes from both intentionally setting aside time and inviting God into "life where ever we are, whatever the situation" (Foster, 2004:223). Despite God's graciousness in meeting us where we are, it does seem essential to also have some non-negotiable disciplines and time seeking solace and realigning our heart with His.

Spiritual formation is a work of the Holy Spirit in us and by nature, something that can take place in any setting. It can be gently etched out over years or formed in the midst of painful ordeals of the body, soul, and spirit. Most often, it is a combination of both over the course of our lives. There is nothing gentle about landing yourself in the midst of a slum community in another culture.

No matter what our intentions, our preparations, our passion level or personalities, it is never a gradual experience. The poverty, the heat, the violence... and the longer you stay, the complexity, the betrayals, the failed hopes... all of this is an affront. It questions not just our values, but also our perception of who God is, who we are, and how we relate to others. And yet here too, in the midst of all the problems, we see grace. Grace in the neighbours who share the small amount they have, grace in the husband who does not hit his wife, grace in a grandma miraculously healed, grace in the kids who finish school, and grace in the love that Christ gives to us, irrespective of our performance on the mission field!

Such extremes of love and hate, brokenness and wholeness, evil and miraculous situations where God breaks through—these push the incarnational worker to choose: What do we cling to? Who holds us fast? Choosing to trust and seek God is a posture we pursue over years, but it is also a choice we make on a daily basis.

Cross-cultural living provides opportunities for growth, especially our awareness of ourselves and the assumptions and values on which we operate. Seeking out community provides accountability and support in these new things. There are, however, many traps we can fall into. We cannot expect the cross-cultural experience to draw us near to God if we are not spending time with Him. Most cross-cultural workers are passionate about sharing God's love with the world; this is why they uprooted themselves in the first place. Greenman reminds us:

> Spiritual formation is our continuing response to the reality of God's grace shaping us into the likeness of Jesus Christ, through the work of the Holy Spirit, in the community of faith, for the sake of the world. (2010:24)

Responding to our identity as God's beloved, a new creation in Christ, can steady us in times of shedding other identity markers that we've valued. Likewise, there is freedom in stepping outside one's culture to evaluate and adopt that which is reflective of the kingdom of God. Moving into the unknown brings an opportunity to step forward in faith and, as we follow the Spirit's nudging, we are able to see God's hand at work around us. Ultimately, our life purpose is to love God and bring glory to His name; He calls us to do so. His greatest call on our lives is to be his children. How then can we not pursue the intimacy this implies!

REFERENCES

Averbeck, Richard E. 2008. "Spirit, Community, and Mission: A Biblical Theology for
    Spiritual Formation". *Journal of Spiritual Formation & Soul Care* 1(1):27–53.

Barker, Ashley. 2003. *Finding Life: Reflections from a Bangkok Slum*. Springvale, Australia: Go
    Alliance.

Barker, Ashley. 2012. *Slum Life Rising: How to Enflesh Hope Within a New Urban World*.
    Dandenong North, Australia: Urban Neighbours of Hope. Kindle Version.

Bessenecker, Scott A., ed. 2010 *Living Mission: The Vision and Voices of the New Friars*.
    Downers Grove, IL: InterVarsity Press.

Brant, Cindy. 2015. "What Living Cross Culturally Taught Me About Being a Christian."
    A Live Overseas: The Missions Conversation. Retrieved May 20, 2015 (http://
    www.alifeoveseas.com/what-living-cross-culturally-taught-me-about-being-a-
    christian).

Bryce, Ruth, Sophal Cheng, and Oddny Gumear. 2015. *MAVP Social Research Project:
    Investigation into Spiritual Practices for Christian Workers*. Melbourne, Australia:
    Tabor College.

Billings, J. Todd. 2012. "The Problem With Incarnational Ministry." Christianity Today 56(7).
    Retrieved May 13, 2015 (http://www.christianitytoday.com/ct/2012/july-
    august/the-problem-with-incarnational-ministry.html).

Corbett, Steve and Brian Fikkert. 2009. *When Helping Hurts: How to Alleviate Poverty Without
    Hurting the Poor and Yourself*. Chicago, IL: Moody Publishers.

Cushner, Kenneth and Richard Brislin. 1986. *Intercultural Interactions: A Practical Guide*.
    Thousand Oaks, CA, Sage Publications.

Duncan, Michael. 2005. *Who Stands Fast: Discipleship in Difficult Places*. Melbourne, Australia:
    UNOH Publishing.

Elmer, Duane. 1993. *Cross-cultural Conflict: Building Relationships for Effective Ministry*.
    Downers Grove, IL: InterVarsity Press.

———. 2006. *Cross-cultural Servanthood: Serving the World in Christlike Humility*. Downers
    Grove, IL: InterVarsity Press.

InterNations. "Defining Culture." Retrieved May 29, 2015 (http://www.internations.org/
    magazine/intercultural-communication-15409/defining-culture-2).

Foster, Richard. 1981. *Freedom of Simplicity*. New York, NY: HarperCollins.

———. 2004. *Streams of Living Water: Celebrating the Great Traditions of Christian Faith*.
    Westbury, UK: Eagle Publishing.

———. 2008. *Life With God: A Life-transforming New Approach to Bible Reading*. London, UK:
    Hodder & Stoughton.

Gardner, Laura Mae. 2013. *Healthy, Resilient and Effective in Cross-cultural Ministry*. Bandung,
    Indonesia: Laura Mae Gardner.

Greenfield, Craig. 2007. *The Urban Halo: A Story of Hope for Orphans of the Poor*. Milton
    Keynes, UK: Authentic Media.

Greenman, Jeffery P. and George Kalantzis. (eds.) 2010. *Life in the Spirit: Spiritual Formation
    in Theological Perspective*. Downers Grove, IL: InterVarsity Press.

Jack, Kristin, ed. 2010. *The Sound of Worlds Colliding: Stories of Radical Discipleship from
    Servants of Asia's Urban Poor*. Phnom Penh, Cambodia: Servants of Asia's Urban
    Poor.

Jones, Jerry. 2015. "The Seven Lies of Living Cross Culturally." *The Culture Blend*. Retrieved
    April 15, 2015 (http://www.thecultureblend.com/the-seven-lies-of-living-cross-
    culturally/).

Kilpin, Juliet. 2013. *Urban to the Core: Motives for Incarnational Mission*. Leistershire, UK: Matador.

Lingenfelter, S. and M. Mayers. 1986. *Ministering Cross-culturally: An Incarnational Model for Personal Relationships*. Grand Rapids, IL: Baker Academic.

Manning, Brennan. 1990. *The Ragamuffin Gospel*. Colorado Springs, CO: Multnomah Publishers.

Matheson, Andy. 2010. *In His Image: Understanding and Embracing the Poor*. Milton Keynes, UK: Authentic Media.

McKnight, Scot. 2010. "The Jesus We Never Knew." *Christianity Today* 54(4):22. Retrieved May 15, 2015 (http://www.christianitytoday.com/ct/2010/April/15.22.html).

Mother Theresa. 1985. *Total Surrender*. Ann Arbor, MI: Servant.

Nouwen, Henri. 1992. *Life of the Beloved: Spiritual Living in a Secular World*. New York, NY: Crossroad.

Parker, Laura. 2012. "10 Reasons Not to Become a Missionary." *A Life Overseas: The Missions Conversation*. Retrieved May 20, 2015 (http://www.alifeoverseas. com/10-reasons-not-to-become-a-missionary).

Pieh-Jones, Rachal. 2013. "Beyond Culture Shock: Culture Pain, Culture Stripping." *A Life Overseas: The Missions Conversation*. Retrieved May 20, 2015 (http://www. alifeoverseas.com/beyond-culture-shock-culture-pain-culture-stripping).

Porterfield, Jackson. 2006. "The Four Greats of Wholistic Ministry." *Servants to Asia's Urban Poor*. Retrieved 15th April 2015 (http:// servantsasia.org/four-greats-wholistic-ministry).

Reed, Naomi. 2009. *Over My Shoulder: Exploring the Impact of Personality on Cross-cultural Missions*. Sydney, Australia: Ark House Press.

Rohr, Richard. 1989. *Discovering the Enneagram*. New York, NY: Crossroad.

Servant Partners. 2017. "Purpose." Retrieved 15th April 2015 (http://www.servantpartners. org/index.php?page=purpose).

Servants to Asia's Urban Poor. 2013. "Servants' Commitment To Belief & Action." Retrieved 15th April 2015 (http://servantsasia.org/who-we-are/what-we-believe).

Shaw, Ryan. 2014. *Spiritual Equipping for Mission: Thriving as God's Message Bearers*. Downer's Grove, IL: InterVarsity Press. Kindle Version.

Smith, T. Aaron. 2012. *Living in the Neighbourhood: Developing a Sustainable Incarnational Ministry Among the Urban Poor*. Pomona, CA: Servant Partners.

Taylor, John. 1972. *The Go-between God: The Holy Spirit and Christian Mission*. London, UK: SCM Press.

Teague, David. 2012. *Godly Servants: Discipleship and Spiritual Formation for Missionaries*. N.p.: Mission Imprints. Kindle Version.

Ten Boom, Corrie. 1971. *The Hiding Place*. Old Tappan, NJ: Fleming H. Revell.

Toan, Pamela. 2012. "Incarnational Ministry – Some Thoughts on How to Maintain a Healthy Spiritual Life." *Spiritual Growth Ministries*. Retrieved 20th May 2015 (http://sgm.org.nz).

Trotter, Elizabeth. 2015a. "I Can't Trust Anyone: Lies We Believe." *A Life Overseas: The Missions Conversation*. Retrieved May 15, 2015 (http://www.alifeoverseas.com/i-cant-trust-anyone-lies-we-believe).

——— 2015b. "God Is Disappointed With Me: Lies We Believe." *A Life Overseas: The Missions Conversation*. Retrieved May 15, 2015 (http://www.alifeoverseas.com/god-is-disappointed-with-me-lies-we-believe).

Wicks, Robert J. 1988. *Living a Gentle, Passionate Life*. Mahwah, NJ: Paulist Press.

Willard, D. 2002. *Renovation of the Heart: Putting on the Character of Christ.* Colorado Springs, CO: NavPress.

Willard, Dallas. N.d. "Spiritual Formation: What It Is, and How It Is Done." Retrieved November 19, 2014 (http://www.dwillard.org/articles/individual/spiritual-formation-what-it-is-and-how-it-is-done).

Websites:

InnerCHANGE: A Christian Order Among the Poor
http://www.innerchange.org

Servant Partners: Transformation Alongside the Urban Poor
http://www.servantpartners.org

Servants to Asia's Urban Poor.
http://servantsasia.org

Urban Neighbours of Hope
http://www.unoh.org

"Being" and "Doing" in an Unjust World

Lee Chee Loi

An examination of the need for effective spiritual formation in Christians working for justice for the poor, and the role of the local congregation and the Christian faith-based NGO in facilitating it.

Spiritual formation talk has emerged from many within both the laity and clergy in evangelical circles. Something deeper is needed, more than the recognised group and individual activities amongst the conservatives, where seemingly all issues of spiritual growth can be dealt with merely through reading, hearing, and preaching the Word of God.

Dallas Willard expressed great concern with such thinking and felt that this led to the "marginalisation of discipleship to Jesus", (2014:2) where we can become Christians without being disciples, with mere soul winning for some or social action for others. Hence the growing hunger for something more that would actually lead to a transformation of life. True Christlikeness needs to be established deep within us, so "we could be the life-transforming salt and light in a darkened world" (Willard, 2014:2–3).

Understanding Spiritual Formation

Christian spiritual formation is the progressive transformation of the human heart, spirit, or will, which results in Christlike deeds done in the power of Christ (Willard, 2014:1). As partakers in the divine nature, Christians are transformed progressively in their character, as seen in 2 Peter 1:4–7. Such progression always concludes with *agape*, as in Colossians 3. Romans 5 concludes with God's love being poured out within our hearts through the given Holy Spirit (verse 5), but it requires our intentional efforts as well as the grace of God (Willard, 2014:1)

Jeffrey Greenman concurs with the essence of Willard's definition of spiritual formation, adding that this transformation is not only in individuals, but also "in the community of faith, for the sake of the world". This increases understanding of the wider context, and also reinforces the fact that our spiritual development must lead to loving actions for others. Greenman emphasises a continuing response to God's grace in shaping us into Christlikeness through the Holy Spirit (Rom. 8:29; 2 Cor. 3:18). This "involves grace-based disciplines of confession, forgiveness, and reconciliation" (Greenman, 2010:24-25), including disciplines like prayer, fasting, meditation, a shared community life of worship, fellowship and teaching, and embracing a 'cruciform' way of life of self-sacrifice and humble service for the sake of others.

This is what Jesus showed in his earthly ministry and told his followers to do (Mark 10:42–45; John 13:12–17; Phil. 2:1–11). (Greenman, 2010:26; cited Gorman, Michael J. 2001 in "Cruciformity: Paul's Narrative Spirituality of the Cross", Grand Rapids: Eerdsman). In Hebrews 12:1, we see that it helps Christians, faced with the pressures of our activist, hurried culture, to run the race with perseverance (Greenman, 2010:24–26).

'Being' and 'Doing'

Being Christ for others, together with friendship and communion with God, is the essential purpose of the Christian life. Our being in the image of God is manifested in our doing, and these cannot be separated. The problem of 'doing' without 'being' is clearly shown in Matthew 7:22–23, where Jesus says that on the last day, he will reject many of the people who thought that they would enter the kingdom of heaven because of all their wonderful deeds.

The problem was that their 'doing' was without any concomitant transformation of their being toward Christlikeness. Likewise, in Matthew 23:27–29, Jesus warned the Pharisees of their hypocrisy. Their external life looked righteous, whilst their internal life was evil and dead. Christlikeness is to be the source from which all genuine 'doing' or mission flows (Mulholland, 2013:15–16).

Community and Praxis

The New Testament shows that following Christ draws us into the messianic community of the disciples of Jesus. In Mark's gospel, we see that those who respond to Jesus' call, he brings into this new community (3:13–35) and then sends them out on a mission to the world (6:7–13). The disciples learned important lessons of life on the road together.

The experience of shared joy and sorrow bound the disciples as a community of God's people as they sought to do God's will. They also realised that what happened to Jesus automatically happened to them. When Jesus was rejected they experienced similar rejection, and when Jesus was invited to the wedding feast in Galilee, they were included too (Luke 9:58). In Matthew 18:10–22, we see the disciples keeping together and there was continual reconciliation within the community of faith with a spirit of openness and forgiveness (Gill, 1989:119, 128–130).

Paul encourages the Colossians to develop virtues of community— mutual kindness, truth telling, forgiveness, and acceptance across traditional barriers of race, culture, and class (Col. 3:14). Love is the primary virtue and community is the primary context, but each individual must own it (Wright, 2010:144). The early church demonstrated an ideal community with a remarkable prayer life, fellowship, complete harmony, and sharing of material possessions (Acts 2:42–47, 4:32–36, 5:12–16);

there were no needy persons among them (Gill, 1989:140).

Our intimacy with Christ is best developed in the context of carrying out our responsibilities together in community. Praxis is not only a way of learning, but also for growing spiritually (Campolo and Darling, 2007:188–190). Malaysian Care (MCare) started a Project Staff development programme, where fresh graduates learned together in community for two years. Their spiritual development came both from time spent in mentoring them and also in the context of ministry, just as Jesus told his disciples in Mark 6:30–31. We took them through Colossians 3:1–17, one of Paul's strong ethical passages with a vision of what Christian virtue and character is all about—'being remade in God's image'. In this passage, we find a rich mutual ministry of the word and a renewal of the mind through love, fellowship, prayer, and mutual Christian support (Wright, 2010:140, 168–169).

The Reign of God, Radical Discipleship and Servanthood

In our 'doing' or mission, we need radical living and action as seen in the life and zeal of John Wesley and the Wesleyan movement that was committed to changing the political and economic institutions of Britain. In Acts 10 and 11, we see how Peter grew in love and desire to follow Jesus and live in new radical ways for God's reign (Campolo and Darling, 2007:51, 54, 72–76). The desire to change the world begins with a desire to change ourselves (Groody, 2007:251).

Daniel Groody describes this kind of spiritual life as ascending the mountain of God in the Transfiguration, where our hearts are transformed, and then descending into the valley of injustice, seeing through the eyes of transformed hearts and engaging people who face injustice around us. Such a descent begins with a conviction of the power of love and a vision of the kingdom, just as Jesus in Philippians 2:5–8 descended to serve the suffering and "humbled himself, becoming obedient to death, even death on a cross" (2007:240–245).

There are many examples. The Simple Way is a group of young 'radicals' who live together in intentional community in a derelict part of Philadelphia, to be with the poor in their brokenness (Claiborne and Campolo. 2013:14). Dorothy Day of The Catholic Worker movement chose to live an insecure life amongst the reality of poverty (Rakoczy, 2006:143), demonstrating radical trust in Christ, who also lived a poor life, often without a place to lay His head (Luke 9:58).

But Christians working for justice for the poor must ensure an attitude of servanthood, as quite often they have superior resources like knowledge and money. Jesus, in all his power and authority, humbled himself like a bondservant to be amongst us (Phil. 2:5–8). His master teaching to his disciples was that in order to lead, we need to be a servant, for even He came to serve (Mark 10:43–45). Jesus' activity in and for the world is totally pervaded by *agape* love and by the renunciation of power. We experience Jesus' presence when we serve "the least of these" (Augsburger, 2006:48–52).

Serving is synonymous with empowering, just as Jesus served and empowered His 12 disciples. Tearfund UK emphasises servanthood and empowering local communities they serve (Frost, 2011:22–23). In MCare, the indigenous community, including women, are empowered to participate in sustainable agriculture development and make decisions in the co-operative movement. This is crucial because often the poor remain poor, as the rich and powerful are not prepared to serve and empower them.

When Young Soon, then leader of MCare's rural community development, first explored ministry amongst the indigenous people, he was told by their leader to "sit down, shut up and listen". He humbly obeyed, listened, prayed and built community for three years. He and his team immersed themselves in the community, demonstrating spirituality rooted in Christlike humility, a virtue which both Andrew Murray and John Calvin consider as the root to a vibrant Christian life (Thomas, 1998:48). Young Soon and his wife later chose to live amongst them and learned their language and culture. Similarly, the grace of humility is worked into our lives through the discipline of service and humility and ensures our flesh is kept in check (Foster, 1988:130)

Fasting and Prayer

Isaiah reminds us that fasting and justice ought to go together (Isa. 58:6–7). This helps create a sense of solidarity with those who are hungry. Fasting strengthens our relationship with God by disciplining our passions. Its goal is flourishing human relationships and the prospering of human life (Groody, 2007:248, 250).

Fasting identifies with the distressed as seen in the Old Testament where it is an expression of grief in mourning or contrition; for example, 1 Samuel 31:13 and 2 Samuel 1:12 (Goldingay, 2009:630). Augustine said that fasting gives greater space to the soul, allowing it the freedom to discover God. Through emptying we are filled with His love, His Spirit and His friendship (Houston, 1989:65).

One of the primary benefits of fasting is that it deepens our prayer life. Prayer allows us to develop intimate conversations with Christ that enable us to abide with Him and know each other as intimate friends (John 15:4). It is the doorway to spiritual growth. Prayer opens us up to the Spirit, who alone can change all that which does not conform to the word and heart of Christ (Rom. 12:2). Moses prayed boldly because he believed his prayers could change things, even God's mind (Ex. 32:14). For people like John Wesley and Martin Luther King, to breathe was to pray. We are challenged to change the world by prayer (Foster, 1988:34–35).

The disciples' devotional and prayerful lives expressed kingdom ways and led to loving others and God more sincerely, as in the early church in Acts 2:42–46 (Houston, 1989:42, 54). The more we pray for God's kingdom to come, the more we compassionately see the injustices of the world and desire to correct them (Stassen and Gushee, 2003:460). It is in Jesus that we find such spontaneous communion with God, combined with a passionate ethical concern for humanity (Taylor, 1972:225).

Christians are dependent on the help of others and must learn how to receive as well as how to give, most of all in the things of the Spirit. "Brothers, pray for us also", says Paul (1 Thess. 5:25; HCSB), and "be my allies in the fight; pray to God for me" (Rom. 15:30; NEB). Likewise, in our tiredness, we learn to 'let go' and 'let God', an important part of prayer (Taylor, 1972:233–235).

We also need to realise that spiritual warfare is real. Paul tells us to put on the armour of God, to "pray in the Spirit on all occasions" and "be alert and always keep on praying for all the Lord's people" (Eph. 6:18). God's power is needed to change because there are things outside human control (James, 2004:22).

The Holy Spirit and Our Prophetic Call

Christian spirituality refers to experiences of being filled with the same Holy Spirit that the apostle Paul talked about in 1 Corinthians 2:12–14, where he emphasised the need to be spiritually filled or formed in order to understand the things of the Spirit as they are spiritually discerned.

Knowing Jesus and being 'born again' involve this kind of transcendent intimacy with God, where revelations of God's love show us the limits of propositional truth. We need a transcendent intimacy with God, as a compassionate desire to work for justice for the poor with human strength alone is limited (Campolo and Darling, 2007:4). My personal experience bears this out. It was through much prayer, including a humbling conviction by the Holy Spirit through an epiphany. The smile of Hannah, a severely disabled client who could not speak, broke my resistance and struggle to answer the call to MCare and I was transformed.

In his first public ministry in Luke 4:18–19, Jesus, who returned from His desert-testing empowered by the Holy Spirit, demonstrated concern for social justice for the poor and oppressed, quoting the prophetic call of Isaiah 61:1–2. The church was birthed at Pentecost, when the Spirit of God came upon the praying disciples. It was the same Spirit that came upon the Old Testament prophets and empowered them often to stand up for God and His kingdom in this world (Averback, 2008:47–51).

It is only when we stand with the poor and oppressed in real situations that we can claim that we stand alongside them in our prayer life (Elliot, 1985:29). Early church believers like Stephen, filled with the Holy Spirit

(Acts 6:1–8), were empowered to serve and exercise Christlikeness (Cole, 2007:245).

The Holy Spirit raises the believers' awareness of the deceit of other gods' pretence to satisfy our deepest longings. It is thus a work of the Holy Spirit that leverages the New Testament warnings to believers against idols (1 John 5:21), storing earthly treasures (Matt. 6:19–21), serving other 'masters' (Luke 6:13), and being conformed to or having friendship with the world (Rom. 12:1). In Ephesians 6:18, Paul exhorts us to pray at all times in the Spirit (Saucy, 2011:151–152).

The Holy Spirit is also responsible for empowering and leading us into mission. If there is to be any human transformation that is sustainable, it will be because of the action of the Holy Spirit, not the effectiveness of our development technology or our smart processes (Myers, 2011:84).

Denying the Spirit's Power

The story of the rich young man in Matthew 19 shows us that he was trying to obey and follow God all in his own strength, as he disciplined himself to obey and follow the Ten Commandments. But when tested on selling all his possessions, it was just too hard for him. He had missed the real purpose of the discipline to selflessly conform to Christlikeness through the power of the Holy Spirit. Jesus told his disciples that whilst doing this is impossible for humans, all things are possible for God (Matt. 19:25–26). In 2 Timothy 3:5, Paul said that he was often guilty of "holding on to the outward form but denying its power", trying to live a spiritual life without the Spirit (Campolo and Darling, 2007:84).

Worshipping God through our own willpower may produce outward success, but in the cracks and crevices of our lives, our deep inner condition will show. Jesus describes this condition when he speaks of the external righteousness of the Pharisees, and tells them that they have to account for the careless words that they will say at some unguarded moment, for "out of the abundance of the heart, the mouth speaks" (Matt. 12:34–36; ESV) and will reveal the true condition of the heart (Foster, 1988:5).

Kingdom Ethics

Jesus reveals that following Him demands ascending to the values, ideals, and ethical demands of the kingdom of God. In order to see the world as God sees it, we must begin to see with the eyes of the heart (Eph. 1:15–21). In Mark 8:31–33, Peter was unable to hear and see clearly when he rebuked Jesus, but Jesus in turn rebuked Peter as He saw the devil's presence and influence (Groody, 2007:240–242).

Christians need training in perception, acquiring a taste for what is being revealed in Jesus, but often our senses are being dulled by sin and we require healing and rehabilitation. On the mountain of transfiguration, Peter tried to possess the glory. In the valley of injustice, he tried to avoid the cross. Jesus even called Peter "Satan" when he tried to stop Jesus from going through the cross, and Jesus had to rebuke him. Peter's propensity for getting it wrong keeps us on our toes (Peterson, 2000:336–337).

In the Sermon on the Mount, Jesus' emphasis is on positive 'transforming initiatives' that give real, practical grace-based guidance for Christian ethics to confront injustices. For example, according to Matthew 5:21–26, whenever we are angry or feel insulted, we should regularly talk things over and seek peace or reconciliation. It is the way of deliverance from vicious cycles of anger and insult. A key part of Jesus' message is repentance, where we name the error and correct it. We cannot assume to ever eliminate all causes of error and vicious cycles in our Christian activism, but through such transforming initiatives there is deliverance from captivity to the vicious cycles. Likewise, in Matthew 5:38–42, we see a vicious cycle of revengeful retaliation, but transforming initiatives, like Martin Luther King's non-violent direct action, oppose injustice, stand up for dignity and invite reconciliation (Stassen and Gushee, 2003:136–141).

Another critical kingdom ethic for Christian disciples must surely be the sanctity of human life. Gushee believes that only God is strong enough to ground the immovable commitment to the sanctity of human life. We are no longer just made in God's image; through the incarnation, God has become one of us, and thus no human being can be seen as worthless nor treated cruelly. When we fall more deeply in love with Christ, we learn to love our neighbours as God loves them (2010:214–221).

Integrity and Authenticity

Jesus said that without Him, we can do nothing (John 15:5), but it is also true that if we do nothing, we will not have Him. Spiritual formation requires us to take wise steps in accomplishing this reality. The hunger of the human heart that is unfed by what is authentic will go for what is unauthentic, destroying itself in the process (Willard, 2014:2–3).

Integrity is a characteristic of God. It has the suggestion of being whole in the sense of being steadfastly committed to what is right or 'blameless', as in Psalm 18:23–3. It is the first quality that Psalm 15 highlights of one who spends time with God (Goldingay, 2009:600).

Job's faith was unwavering. In Job 13, he affirmed God's justice, not tolerating his sufferings despite an authentic life of integrity and innocence, and says that if he dies, he would present his case to God (Job 13:18). At his lowest point (Job 19:23–29), he could still say "My Redeemer lives" (13:25; ESV), reflecting and demonstrating the need for a strong faith and personal relationship with God when subjected to suffering (Fiorello, 2011:173).

This is something that Christians must expect, as seen in the suffering of the Messiah himself and the apostles like Paul at the hands of zealous Jews and pagan authorities. Such suffering develops character (Wright, 2010:177). Peter said that our faith would be tested, just as gold is refined in fire (1 Peter 1:7).

Faith, Trust and Dependence on God

Faith in God is trust in God's character, sovereignty, and ultimate triumph. In view of the brokenness of the world, Satan's continued victories and life's many disappointments, we can easily lose heart and trust in God, and look to other idols or objects of trust. Jesus warned that we should not entrust our holy and valuable things, like our trust and loyalty, to the world.

In Matthew 6:1–33, he tells us to trust God rather than human recognition, prestige, or money. Matthew 7:6 tells us to trust God rather than the ruling Roman powers of the time. Jesus was not saying that we will get everything we ask for in prayer, but that God is faithful and deserves our trust, unlike worldly idols (Stassen and Gushee, 2003:456–459).

Biblical change begins with God's vision, just as the Exodus vision of escape came from God to Moses in a burning bush. Even Jesus said that "the Son can do only what he sees the Father doing" (John 5:19). Although God is the author of change, He also chose humans to be co-creators with him of change. The major changes in both Old and New Testament began with God entrusting the work to humans, for example, Abraham, Joseph, Moses, Joshua, Peter, John and Paul. Characterised by their humility and their attitude of servant leadership that enabled them to be used by God, they constantly listened to God and sought His presence to transform situations. Moses' prayer is a good example: "If your Presence does not go with us, do not send us up from here." (Ex. 33:15)

Yet, as humans, there is a tendency to take responsibility away from God, as Moses did when he tried to solve Israel's problem in his own strength by killing the Egyptian slave master. Paul highlights this tendency when he challenged the Galatian church: "Are you so foolish? After beginning with the Spirit, are you now trying to attain your goal by human effort?" (James, 2004:21–23). Human beings are to be God's co-creators in the world, empowered by God to create out of everything that God created. But we must remember that the purpose of our creating is to enable the well-being of all humans and the natural world. In this, we are dependent on God's empowerment. God brings the kingdom, not us. We cannot carry the weight of building the kingdom on our own shoulders (Myers, 2011:61, 77).

FACILITATING SPIRITUAL FORMATION

Given this critical need for effective spiritual formation for Christians working for justice for the poor, it is important to explore how churches and Christian NGOs can facilitate it.

Intentional Discipleship

When Dallas Willard enquired of many church and para-church groups what their plans were for putting to death "whatever belongs to your earthly nature" (Col. 3:5), he did not receive any positive response. He believes the church needs to have an avid discipleship in Christ that brings the inward transformation of thought, feeling, and character (2006:15, 84), that "cleanses the inside of the cup" (Matt. 23:25–26; BLB) and "make[s] the tree good" (Matt. 12:33, BLB). Intentional discipleship was the major reason for MCare's project staff programme, as mentioned above.

Small Groups for Community and Praxis

All Christians who are members of God's household, the church, should be a spiritually-transforming community, which is to "spur one another on toward love and good deeds" and "encourage one another" (Heb. 10:24–25) as Christ was sent to love people (Averback, 2008:43–45).

The class meetings that John Wesley instituted provided the setting for 'eldering', the ministry of watching over one another. Converts were divided into small groups that met weekly for mutual accountability and support (Foster, 2005:185). Many churches have formed 'care groups' with the same purpose. The widespread popularity of small groups in churches today demonstrates the need for this kind of support, and the potential for a renewal of the church through community (Gill, 1989:148).

Building a Culture that Nurtures Ideals of Kingdom Living, Service and Ethics

Integrating Faith and Spirituality into the Organisation

It is the challenge of leadership to try to build a culture that nurtures the ideals of Christian living, service, and ethical behaviour. To do that, faith and spirituality should be integrated into the organisation, as increasing secularism tends to bring about the subjective validation of moral and ethical positions.

For example, our core documents must reflect our spiritual or faith foundations. World Vision sees its ministry as "an expression of the Church" (Mitchell, 2011:15, 21). MCare sees its ministry as "a calling to be the visible expression of the wholistic mission of Christ..." (MCare Policies, 2003:3).

Creating Space for Grace

By integrating our Christian faith with our professional practice, we create more space for God's grace to transform people and organisations. This was illustrated in the remarkable transformation story of the Tangababwe Christian Fellowship, where faithful prayer, listening to God and the divine grace and power of God brought repentance and forgiveness to a divided and corrupt organisation.

Faith gave them a transformed identity. They became more relational, united and productive and regained respect (James, 2004:8, 30–35). When such faith integration into NGO management occurs, leaders need humility, wisdom, and integrity to live out the virtues they encourage in others (James, 2010:266).

Ensure Reflection, Listening and Prayer

In our Christian activist journey, we often fail to leave room for God's spirit. We need space for reflection and relational conversations.

Rick James highlights that reflection is a critical step in spiritual development, quoting the example of the appointment of the youngest Bishop in Kenya, which went against the will of the powerful church leaders in the Diocese. But the Bishop organised spiritual retreats of contemplation and meditation for the leadership, which enabled them to put right their relationships with God and with one another. This led to transformational healing of the conflict and renewal of friendships (2004:39–41).

Likewise, the church should invest more time and effort in reflection, on issues like the role of a transformative spirituality within the context of their mission. Such reflection helps us see or find the correlation between the deeper longings of our heart and the structures of organised religion (Groody, 2009:260).

The disciples' devotional and prayerful life expressed kingdom ways and led to loving others and God more sincerely as in the early church in Acts 2:42–46 (Houston, 1989:42, 54). The more we pray for God's kingdom to come, the more we compassionately see the injustices of the world and desire to correct them (Stassen and Gushee, 2003:460). It is in Jesus that we find such spontaneous communion with God, combined with passionate ethical concern for humanity (Taylor, 1972:225). In addition to normal scheduled prayer meetings, churches could participate in events like the Micah 10.10 global prayer for poverty eradication, which received strong support in Malaysia.

Tearfund UK's inspirational document on its future direction calls for a Christ-centred, values-based organisation. It came about largely because of its CEO Matthew Frost's week-long time of reflecting and listening to God. Frost committed to increasing the organisation's emphasis on prayer, as "prayer is the heart of our Christian distinctive" (Frost, 2011:1, 12). In my visit to Tearfund UK, I saw that the staff faithfully begin work with prayer and devotion time. We do that in MCare too. We also have a specially designed prayer room to facilitate prayer for staff at any time needed.

Provide Servant Leadership and Pastoral Care

Some have described dysfunctional management in organisations as lack of love. There is now an increasing emphasis on servant leadership, brought about by leaders and authors like Greenleaf and Blanchard, with a focus on love and service to stakeholders (James, 2010:261). Stott reminds us that Christian leaders are to serve the interests of others in Christlikeness, and rejoice in humble and joyful service (1984/2006:493–494).

Matthew Frost encourages his team to abide in Christ with servant-hearted relationships, explaining that it is both a personal and corporate discipline. This implies giving more space and energy to prayer, encouraging each other in discipleship, intentionally seeking the presence of God to guide and direct their actions, and aspiring to be servants just as Jesus came to serve (2011:16–17).

MCare encourages partner churches to 'commission' their members who join us. This heightens awareness in staff's own churches of the importance of prayer support and pastoral care. For example, Young Soon's sending church sees him and his wife as their 'missionaries'. The church prays and cares about their spiritual development and the spiritual support they receive from the local church in their mission field.

Equipping and Developing

Whether directly or indirectly, the whole of Scripture contributes to the understanding and practice of spirituality and spiritual formation (Averback, 2008:30). As Paul puts it in Ephesians 4:12, God gave pastors and teachers to the church to equip and support the people in their ministry and formation. The church should help build a biblical worldview for sustaining Christian ethical witness and encourage believers to "seek the welfare of the city" where God has put them (Wright, 2010:272).

Dietrich Bonhoeffer saw clearly Hitler's injustice and acted courageously against it when others failed to do so because he was converted and shaped by Jesus' Sermon on the Mount (Stassen and Gushee, 2003:126). We need a robust recovery of the deepest theological reasons for those moral beliefs that lead us to defend the dignity of our suffering neighbour. And that kind of work can only begin in the church (Groody, 2007:219).

But typical patterns of evangelical engagement with Scripture can easily devolve into an information-oriented rationalism, where the Bible is not absorbed and digested in a more deeply transformative manner. Thus, there is a need for reaffirmation of the central place of the Bible in evangelical spiritual nurture and teaching, and an open-minded re-examination of the ways in which the Bible is studied and taught to and with congregations (Greenman, 2010:28–29). For example, the average adult Sunday School class is far too superficial and devotional to help us study the Bible, although there are exceptions and some churches offer serious Bible courses (Foster, 1988:69).

The lack of available training at tertiary level in development from a Christian perspective, even in a country like Australia, has hindered the practice and integration of Christian faith into Christian development organisations (Mitchell, 2011:13). But it is heartening that the Master of Transformational Development programme offered by Eastern College Victoria in partnership with AGST Alliance and MCare is one initiative that the church and Christian NGOs are facilitating. Whether it is a local church or ministry organisation or a seminary, we must commit ourselves to training in spirituality, along with biblical and theological education (Averback, 2008:45).

The board of a Christian NGO is the primary sponsor and protector of its faith identity. It is critical to invest in the development of board and executive staff by training them as Christian thinkers and leaders. There should be intentional policies and governance processes around faith issues (Mitchell, 2011:8). These are equally relevant for the leadership of churches, which often are overly dependent on merely the pastor for equipping.

Churches and Christian NGOs can make use of their expertise or facilities and help reduce cost in relevant spiritual formation modules, like what is done at the Eastern College MTD programme. Those in more developed nations could contribute to initiatives like this directly, or seek to mobilise their contacts to help financially and enable more scholarships for poorer students to join these courses/modules, contributing to their sustainability.

CONCLUSION

Effective spiritual formation in Christians working for justice for the poor can be likened to a journey made on the 'two feet' of love of God and love of neighbour (Luke 10:27). The unity between the love of God and love of neighbour provides the depth and richness of soil that grows the desire to transform the world of injustice. These two priorities are interdependent. Whilst loving neighbour is a true act of love of God, it is not an explicit act without a living faith. "Thus the activist is called also to the same dynamic: conversion, self-emptying, suffering, surrender, purification, the nights of finding oneself in God—in the midst of the praxis of transforming love" (Rakoczy, 2006:205). This needs to be done with the critical support, love, and servant-leadership of the church and Christian NGOs.

The sufferings and weaknesses of Christians in the present age and tensions of the 'already' and 'not yet' can be challenging, but Romans 8:17–27 reminds us that the Spirit is our sustainer and surety of the kingdom's culmination (Saucy, 2011:103–104).

References

Augsburger, David. 2006. *Dissident Discipleship: A Spirituality of Self-Surrender, Love of God, and Love of Neighbour*. Grand Rapids, MI: Brazos Press.

Averbeck, Richard E. 2008. "Spirit, Community, and Mission: A Biblical Theology for Spiritual Formation." *Journal of Spiritual Formation & Soul Care* 1(1):27–53.

Campolo, Tony and Shane Claiborne. 2012. *Red Letter Christianity: Living the Words of Jesus No Matter the Cost*. London, UK: Hodder & Stoughton.

Campolo, Tony and Mary Albert Darling. 2007. *The God of Intimacy and Action: Reconnecting Ancient Spiritual Practices, Evangelism and Justice*. San Francisco, CA: Jossey-Bass.

Cole, Graham A. 2007. *He Who Gives Life: The Doctrine of the Holy Spirit*. Wheaton, IL: Crossway Books.

Elliott, Charles. 1985. *Praying the Kingdom: Towards a Political Spirituality*. London: Darton, Longman & Todd.

Fiorello, Michael D. 2011. "Aspects of Intimacy With God in the Book of Job." *Journal of Spiritual Formation & Soul Care* 4(2):155–184.

Foster, Richard J. 1988. *Celebration of Discipline: The Pathway to Spiritual Growth*. New York, NY: HarperCollins.

Frost, Matthew. 2011. *New Wineskins: a Christ-centred, Values-based Organization*. Unpublished paper, courtesy of the author.

Gill, Athol. 1989. *Life on the Road: The Gospel Basis for a Messianic Lifestyle*. Homebush West, Australia: Lancer Books.

Goldingay, John. 2009. *Old Testament Theology, vol. 3, Israel's Life*. Downers Grove, IL: Inter-Varsity Press.

Greenman, Jeffrey P. 2010. "Spiritual Formation in Theological Perspective." Pp. 23–35 in *Life in the Spirit: Spiritual Formation in Theological Perspective*, edited by Jeffrey P. Greenman and George Kalantzis. Downers Grove, IL: InterVarsity Press.

Groody, Daniel G. 2007. *Globalization, Spirituality & Justice*. Maryknoll, NY: Orbis Books.

Gushee, David. 2010. "Spiritual Formation & the Sanctity of Life." Pp. 213–226 in *Life in the Spirit: Spiritual Formation in Theological Perspective*, edited by Jeffrey P. Greenman and George Kalantzis. Downers Grove, IL: InterVarsity Press.

Houston, James. 1989. *Prayer the Transforming Friendship*. Oxford, UK: Lion.

James, Rick. 2004. *Creating Space for God's Grace: God's Power in Organizational Change*. Swedish Mission Council. Retrieved February 19, 2013 (http://missioncouncil. se.loopiadns.com/wp-content/uploads/2011/05/04).

James, Rick. 2010. "Managing NGOs With Spirit." Pp. 255–266 in *Management: The Earthscan Companion*, edited by Alan Fowler and Chiku Malunga. London, UK: Earthscan.

Malaysian CARE's (MCARE) Policies 2003.

Mitchell, Bob. 2011. *Becoming a Faithfully-based organization*. Unpublished paper used with permission of author.

Mulholland, Robert M. 2013. "Spiritual Formation in Christ and Mission with Christ." *Journal of Spiritual Formation & Soul Care* 6(1):11–17.

Myers, Bryant. 2011. *Walking With the Poor: Principles and Practices of Transformational Development*. Maryknoll, NY: Orbis Books.

Peterson, Eugene H. 2000. "St. Mark: The Basic Text for Christian Spirituality." Pp. 327–338 in *Exploring Christian Spirituality: An Ecumenical Reader*, edited by Kenneth J. Collins. Grand Rapids, MI: Baker Books.

Rakoczy, Susan. 2006. *Great Mystics and Social Justice: Walking on the Two Feet of Love*. Mahwah, NJ: Paulist Press.

Saucy, Mark R. 2011. "Regnum Spiriti: The Role of the Spirit in the Social Ethics of the Kingdom." *Journal of the Evangelical Theological Society* 54(1):89–108.

Stassen, Glen H. and David P. Gushee. 2003. *Kingdom Ethics: Following Jesus in Contemporary Context*. Downers Grove, IL: IVP Academic.

Stott, John. 2006. *Issues Facing Christians Today*. Grand Rapids, MI: Zondervan.

Taylor, John V. 1972. *The Go-between God: The Holy Spirit and Christian Mission*. London, UK: SCM Press.

Thomas, Gary L. 1998. *The Glorious Pursuit: Embracing the Virtues of Christ*. Colorado Springs, CO: NavPress.

Willard, Dallas. 2006. *The Great Omission: Reclaiming Jesus's Essential Teachings on Discipleship*. New York, NY: HarperCollins.

Willard, Dallas. N.d. "Spiritual Formation: What It Is, and How It Is Done." Retrieved November 19, 2014 (http://www.dwillard.org/articles/individual/spiritual-formation-what-it-is-and-how-it-is-done).

Wright, C. J. H. 2010. *The Mission of God's People: A Biblical Theology of the Church's Mission*. Grand Rapids, MI: Zondervan.

Wright, N. T. 2010. *After You Believe: Why Christian Character Matters*. New York, NY: HarperCollins.

Yelling at God About Poverty

Clinton Bergsma

An introductory exploration of the possible contribution
of lament to community development.

The spiritual practice of lament has largely been overlooked in modern times. When it has been championed, its flag has almost exclusively been raised in the area of Christian worship. While there is increasing interest among Christian psychologists and theologians in the use of lament as a process of dealing with grief and trauma, as yet there appears to have been little exploration of lament's potential contribution to dealing with issues of poverty.

Drawing from Biblical scholarship, theology, psychology and community development commentators, this paper makes a case for the unique contribution of lament to the task of poverty alleviation. Almost the entire global south sees the spiritual as integral to life and thus situations of poverty naturally raise questions of theodicy.

My argument will be that lament addresses these questions while simultaneously being a process for dealing with grief and loss. Lament offers itself as a powerful and appropriate tool for healing and restoration in situations of poverty.

LAMENT AND THE HISTORICAL PEOPLE OF GOD

Lament in the Biblical Narrative

Although largely neglected by the modern Christian community, the practice of lament in the biblical narrative is integral to the experience of God's people (Westermann 1981:263). So many voices cried out in frustration and despair to a God who seemed to have removed himself from the crisis at hand: Moses, David, Elijah, Jeremiah and Job, to name but a few. The biblical narrative never attempts to hide the awkward things that suffering and confused people said about God to God (Broyles 2008:395); a brutal honesty is permitted and remains uncensored from the first page to its last (Westermann 1981:264).

The Exodus event, so prominent in the Hebrew mind, began with a cry of lament (Brueggemann 1995a:106), and the crucifixion, *the* biblical event, hears no less than Jesus cry out with a loud, confused and pained voice: "My God, my God, why have you forsaken me?" Though salvation always begins with a lament in the biblical narrative (Brueggemann 199599), the repeated cries of the historical people of God remain largely unheard and unjoined by 21st-century Christians (Westermann 1981:264f).

Yet if lament is prevalent throughout the biblical narrative and immediately preceded Jesus' death and resurrection—God's climactic intervention into the broken human condition—then surely it has something to teach us about who God is, how the divine-human relationship is to be worked out, and how humanity can be healed. Lament is not a footnote in the story of God's restorative work; it is an indispensable thread woven throughout the narrative.

YAHWEH AND LAMENT

Against God to God

Perhaps one of the most striking features of lament is that it is a complaint to Yahweh about Yahweh; it paradoxically "clings to God against God"

(Westermann 1981:273). Lament asserts that God has not acted as he should have, but it cannot see any other place to bring that complaint other than into the presence of Yahweh himself, and as such is a movement *towards* God (Westermann 1981:273).

Lament maintains God as lover (at times tenuously) while also bringing into question whether this is how lovers truly act (Cohen 2013:52). Lament looks at what is happening in light of the promises and abilities of God, declares with brutal honesty that things are not as they should be, and that frankly, Yahweh cannot wash his hands of the matter (Broyles 2008:395; Brueggemann 1995b:101).

Prayers of invocation, then, assume that God is interested in the unfolding drama. They recognise that the world isn't right; that injustice and oppression are rife; that this sorrow, confusion, this anger and despair *must* be voiced (Cohen 2013:67), and that Yahweh *must* listen and act.

Lament cannot be a mere appendix to a relationship with God; rather it is an inevitable outcome for people who experience the brokenness of life in the company of a Friend and Father who is able to intervene, and has promised to do so. Avoiding lament is to live in either denial of the injustice that exists (Brueggemann 1995b:102) or to attempt some illusion of a relationship with God. Like most illusions, it will be shown for what it is when a slight mishap occurs in the glossy routine.

A God Who is Willing to Listen

How beautiful the imminence of this transcendent God, who is the only one big enough to fix our complaint, and is also willing to hear it (DeGroat 2009:188)! "There is no god like Yahweh" was the catch cry of ancient Israel, but there is also no one who listens like Yahweh. When we lament, "we seek an audience with the most-high God" and he willingly condescends—even if our complaint is irrational, unjust, tainted with self-righteous anger or tarnished with hypocrisy (Broyles 2008:394).

It is poignant that the editors of the Psalter never sought to sanitise or censor the material of the complaints. Rather, the inclusion of lament throughout the biblical canon is indicative of a God who hears his people, hope that "the infants of my enemies would be smashed upon the rocks" (Psalm 139), and *permits* rather than discourages such language (Cohen 2013:79), even though his desire is that they extend love even to their enemies (Matthew 5:43-48).

Yahweh is not only big enough to restore all things; he is big enough to *hear* all things. He listens to the complaints of his bride and gives her room to scream her unfair tirades at him, for he is not indifferent to her suffering; Yahweh has had his share of grief.

A God Acquainted with Sorrow

Indeed, Yahweh is "a God acquainted with grief and sorrow" (Brueggemann 1984:52). He has not stood immune to the suffering of his beloved creation. The impact of the Fall was not confined to the created order; God himself was touched. Perhaps for the first time in all eternity, the heart of God was pierced with pain and regret (Genesis 6:6), and the suffering continued outside the beautiful confines of the Garden of Eden.

The pursuit of his beloved into a world of darkness was often done with pleading lament—Yahweh imploring his people time and time again through the prophets to return to his loving embrace (e.g. Hosea 2). While the Psalms describe humanity's cries to a patient, listening God, the prophets detail Yahweh's pleas with an impassionate, disinterested and fickle humanity. Later in the narrative, it was no longer just his heart that was pierced, but his hands and feet: Humiliated and abandoned by Father and friends, it is fitting that Jesus cried out—with so many who have lamented—those heart-wrenching words of Psalm 22: "My God, my God, why have you forsaken me?"

It is no wonder, then, that lament ultimately draws us closer to Yahweh. This is important. Yahweh not only permits and listens to our complaints, and is able to act on them, but he understands and identifies with the very grieving of our hearts, and it is this symphony that allows lament to be such a powerful healing process.

A Time to Lament

While some scholars have attempted to place the individual psalms of lament in their correct historical context, the task has proved elusive and tenuous (Lasor, Hubbard, and Bush 1996:431f). While this may be an exegetical dilemma for some, a unique benefit is that the psalms take on an abiding quality; their expressions of the ups and downs of the divine-human relationship are not tied to any one place and situation (Cohen 2013:11). While there is a particular linguistic and cultural flavour to them, which importantly grounds them in the history of humanity and prevents them from becoming an abstract ideology, the questions and sentiments they posit are timeless (Hankle 2010:276). These songs of distress provide words for those whose hearts have been too numbed by pain to speak, their voices hoarse from crying.

Laments also express a wide range of sentiments and situations in the divine-human relationship: Anger, despair, questioning, confusion; some individual, some corporate (Broyles 2008:385); some in the context of worship, others in the context of daily life and natural disasters (Brueggemann 1995a:76). When all the biblical laments are placed together, it seems that there are no issues or situations outside the boundaries of lament (Brueggemann 1984:52; Cohen 2013:6). When God's promises appear impotent in light of the world we live in, whatever the context may be, lament is an appropriate process for addressing the predicament.

The Enabling Gift of Lament

Healing Through Screaming

Lament's first enabling gift is the granting of a necessary permission, as Hicks describes it, to 'scream' (Hicks 1993:134). It is well accepted by psychological experts that disclosing emotional trauma directly improves mental and physical health (Pennebaker and Beall 1986:274; Westen, Burton, and Kowalski 2006:398, 588; Lepore, Fernandez-Berrocal, Ragan, and Ramos 2004:341). In contrast, suppressing the emotional outworking of our distress has a negative impact on mental and physical health while also stopping us from moving forward and making meaning of what has occurred (Hicks 1993:34f; Snow, McMinn, Bufford, and Brendlinger 2011:131; Benner, 1990:68; Ringma 2000:104).

As one PTSD[1] sufferer who served as a soldier in East Timor said, "... you're paying for it [emotionally] at the time; it's just on credit. Once you're out of the situation and you let the façade down, it's payday" (Summerton and Wishart 2004; see also Hicks 1993:8). Interestingly, a recent study has suggested that the health benefits of emotional disclosure can be enhanced when people are provided 'response training' (Konig, Eonta, and Dyal 2014). While emotional disclosure is important to mental and physical healing, having a structured process further leverages its benefits.

Lament permits the initial and at times repeated 'scream' that is fundamental to healing from situations of distress, while also providing a framework and a process through which the healing can occur. It is significant that the social sciences are uncovering truths about healing that have long been present in the ancient practice of lament.

As a Movement

While despair, trauma, suffering and theological conundrums often cause us to freeze, circle or wander aimlessly, lament is a process that allows us to move forward without abandoning those feelings or the chaos that ensues (Brueggemann 1984:54). There is a wonderful paradox here, as David Cohen aptly describes:

> The shape, or structure, of psalms of distress can be viewed as juxtaposed to the lack of structure, or containment, often resulting from personal distress. In this way these psalms offer an engagement which paradoxically invites the distressed person to embrace the chaos caused by distress *through* a structure. (2013:35)

---

[1]   Post-traumatic Stress Disorder.

Grieving is never a straightforward process (Benner 1990:72), and while there are loosely recognised stages of grief, most people do not move through them in a sequential, orderly fashion (Worden 2001:25).

Resolution is not always a straightforward phenomenon: While there is a "sense that mourning can be finished... there is also a sense in which mourning is never finished" (Worden 2001:47). Lament provides a framework through which emotional trauma can be expressed, while also moving the participant, even with tidal emotions, towards a place of resolution (Hankle 2010:276).

Lament allows the necessary emotional disclosure while providing a process through which healing can take place. To stagnate at the scream would be harmful, and not just for the larynx. There must be movement (even if it is tidal) towards healing, but without rushing the healing process (Benner 1990:73). Lament, and particularly the regular use of lament, provides the carefully balanced framework that healing from distressful situations requires.

Holding Truths in Tension

It must be pointed out that lament does not always result in resolution; at times the resolution is partial. However, lament enables the distressed person to 'hold' the suffering. Cohen undertook a small study using lament as the process through which unresolved grief was expressed. While none of the 12 participants felt that their particular situation had been resolved, they all experienced a decrease in distress, leading Cohen to suggest that, "This... underlines the significance of lament as a process for *holding* distress rather than, necessarily, *resolving* it" (Cohen 2013:145, 80).

The holding of distress rather than its removal is a consistent conclusion to the laments in the biblical account. Job never received answers to his questions, and no doubt the memories of his dead children and that fateful day remained long after the conclusion of the narrative; yet chapter 42:3 finds Job describing a peace and a deeper understanding of God and his own self. This is *prior* to the positive concluding section where Job receives riches and children again (42:10f). His words were not fatalistic as much as a strangely joyful acceptance that there was something "too wonderful for me" going on (Job 42:3; see also Psalm 10, 22, 55).

Some may argue this is a type of 'meaning making' or 'suspended growth' (Bowlby, in Worden 2001:35), yet I would suggest that there is a delicate difference. Meaning has not been made—"I still don't understand why God let this happen"—yet growth has somehow continued—"I feel less distress." The difference is subtle, yet important. 'Holding distress' allows the lamenter to preserve a number of truths in tension, including the truth that "I don't understand how these truths fit together," while also assisting the person lamenting to have hope and move forward in life. This is a subtle yet significant contribution of lament to situations of distress.

A Working Definition of Lament

Lament then, is a dynamic, yet structured spiritual process of dealing with loss that enables the distressed person to express the full gamut of chaotic emotions that trauma causes, while moving the lamenter towards a resolution, with the entire process undertaken in the empathetic presence of all-powerful Yahweh.

Although lament does not always resolve the issue at hand, it enables the concerned person to 'hold' their distress without abandoning their faith. Lament's close parallels with secular approaches to trauma recovery suggest that expected outcomes can include mental and physical health improvement, coupled with a more intimate relationship with the Divine.

We now begin to explore the potential contribution of the process of lament to the community development sector, focusing on three key contingents: Those experiencing poverty in the global south, the Christian community in the global north, and the community development practitioner.[2]

---

[2] It is my hope that exploring lament for these three key people groups will provide some conversation starters for the role of lament for other important areas of community development (e.g. marketing material, organisational staff care). There is simply not enough space here for a thorough exploration of all areas of community development.

LAMENT AND THE GLOBAL SOUTH

The Broader Impacts of Poverty

It is universally accepted that poverty has an adverse effect on human flourishing. In tackling this issue, western aid and development organisations typically separate the physical and spiritual realms and implement interventions that focus entirely on physical deficiencies (Myers 1999:4f). It should be noted that Christian development organisations are not immune to this dichotomy (Myers 1999:7). However, almost all indigenous cultures and peoples of the global south see life as completely interconnected (Ife, 2013:97f). When disaster strikes or generation after generation experiences poverty in this setting, there are necessarily deep spiritual questions that arise (Myers 1999:87; Aten 2012:132f; Ife and Tesoriero 2006:237).

Further, the impact of poverty extends beyond the tangible needs of the poor and affects mental health (Funk, Epping-Jordan, Drew, Faydi, and Saraceno 2010:28ff). I have met people in rural Indonesia who have buried two, sometimes three children from preventable diseases. One cannot remain unaffected by repeated trauma, and the impact of poverty on mental health often expresses itself through coping behaviours such as addiction, violence and crime (Murali and Oyebode 2004:216f; Trudgen 2000:59, 172f).

However, there are few development organisations that include mapping mental health as a part of needs assessment. Indeed, the impact of poverty on mental health is a relatively new field of inquiry for aid and development organisations (Funk et al. 2010:24; Murali and Oyebode 2004:217).

If poverty causes issues of spirituality, and the trauma it creates leads to mental health issues, then failing to acknowledge and address these foundational poverty outcomes will have unintended consequences for the community development program and the people these programs aim to assist.

Failure to Lament

While it is potentially harmful to attempt programs that ignore local spirituality, passing over the spiritual *questions* of communities can be especially counterproductive, particularly for communities where "life outside of the spiritual context is meaningless and pointless" (Ife and Tesoriero 2006:247).

In these situations, ignoring the spiritual questions raised by poverty or disaster amounts to not just missing part of the story, but at times the *whole* story (Aten 2012:132). Programs built on such a foundation will be woefully inadequate, and the ideals of local participation and ownership, so crucial to sustainable development (Chambers 1983:168ff; Ife 2013:173), will likely be missed or reduced. Space must be created for the spiritual and its theodicean questions when engaging communities that acknowledge spirituality.

In a similar fashion to the issue of bypassing the importance of spirituality, a recent World Health Organisation study found that mental health has largely been overlooked in the community development sector, even though 80% of the mental health burden is found in low and middle-income countries (Funk et al. 2010:24). Although incidents of depression (3.2%) among the poor are only slightly lower than cases of malaria (4%), malaria receives significantly more attention and resources (Funk et al. 2010:2). Failing to address the mental health burden of poverty runs the risk of the mentally ill remaining in their perilous state, sinking further into greater vulnerability, and dying prematurely (Funk et al. 2010:24).

If the trauma of experiencing disaster and poverty has a strong correlation to issues of theodicy, and if failing to disclose that emotional trauma causes high rates of mental health issues among global south communities, then lament is well placed to contribute significantly to the transformational program.

The Potential Contribution of Lament

Spiritual and emotional care in development and disaster relief must be suitable to the particular spiritual worldview of the community being engaged, and must not be 'parachuted in' from the global north context (Aten 2012:132f). However, this does not imply that principles cannot be taken from a process such as lament and appropriately contextualised; the use of Middle Eastern lament in the global north demonstrates its adaptability across cultures.

Lament is unique in that it is a process that has distinct parallels with modern approaches to grief and trauma counselling, yet uses this process to heal and empower in the context of the divine-human relationship (Cohen 2013:65; see also Snow et al. 2011:133) so important to the majority of global south communities.[3]

Lament enables a person to move to a place of peace even when the situation at hand has not yet resolved, which is a regular phenomenon in situations of poverty. While a government or development agency may improve a particular community's access to water (for example), issues such as education, conflict and the local economy may remain relatively unaltered. Life has improved, but it is still incredibly difficult; everything desired has not yet been received, and so an element of distress continues.

However, regular lament has the potential to enable people in poverty to hold that continuing distress in tension without their worldview or spirituality crumbling. This is crucial for communities of faith, without which hope may be lost and coping behaviours of addiction, violence and crime may return. The evidence of lament working in this way is perhaps most clearly seen by the African-American slaves, who used lament effectively in the face of continuing hardship and oppression:

> I am a poor pilgrim of sorrow
> I'm tossed in this wide world alone
> No hope I have for tomorrow;
> I've started to make heaven my home.

---

[3]   A number of authors interestingly noted the prevalence of the question of theodicy among agnostics, suggesting that lament may be a useful tool at times among communities that don't express a particular faith per se (Hicks 1993:106; Snow et al. 2011:131; Exline and Grubbs 2011:306).

> Sometimes I am tossed and driven, Lord,
> Sometimes I don't know where to roam.
> I've heard of a city called heaven,
> I've started to make it my home.

Lament, if not already used by suffering communities of faith, has the potential to contribute significantly to their empowerment, healing and holding of distress. As yet, it appears to be underutilised, but perhaps with the rising recognition of the importance of spirituality and mental health issues in situations of poverty, the social sciences and community development theorists may uncover the process of lament as an important and appropriate community engagement tool.

Lament and the Christian global north

The Disconnect

While the inclusion of a section exploring lament and the Christian global north in the context of community development may appear out of place, it is this very assumption that requires addressing. The underlying axiom is that the Christian global north can be separated from their southern family. This separation ignores the repeated and consistent biblical mandate to care for the poor and vulnerable. While most Christians make the odd donation to their favourite aid organisation, there is little difference in overall posture towards the poor between those who describe themselves as 'deeply religious' and those who would call themselves 'non-religious' (Sider 1997:40).

Issues of social justice are not at the forefront of many Christian communities; we have somehow managed to have a "pious spirit" while ignoring the "real world" (Stassen and Gushee 2003:449). As Brueggemann succinctly puts it:

> It is a curious fact that the church has, by and large, continued
> to sing songs of orientation in a world increasingly experienced
> as disoriented. That may be laudatory. It could be that such

relentlessness is an act of bold defiance... a great evangelical "nevertheless"... but... it is my judgement that this action of the church is less an evangelical defiance guided by faith, and much more a frightened, numb denial and deception that does not want to acknowledge or experience the disorientation of life. The reason for such relentless affirmation of orientation seems to come, not from faith, but from the wishful optimism of our culture (1984:51).

Though Brueggemann is exploring the reasons for the avoidance of lament in the liturgy of the modern western church, it is striking how complementary his thoughts are to those of Sider, Stassen and Gushee.

For the vast majority of humanity, the world is a "frightening and disorienting" place, particularly for the poor and vulnerable. But the modern Christian is permitted to dance to only one band, Enlightenment optimism, and its lead vocalist, the marketing jingle, while the dissenting body of theodicy lies bound, gagged and hidden out of sight behind an overworked smoke machine, though her voice sings truer than any other. Modernity primarily births Christians who must not lament or show doubt, as it may be indicative of an impermissible crack in the proverbial armour of God (Brueggemann 1995:102f; Brueggemann 1984:52).

In a recent American study by Exline and Grubb, 52 per cent of people who disclosed their anger towards God with a friend said the response they received was that "it is wrong to have negative feelings towards God" (2011:310). There is little room in the modern Christian mind for confusion, doubt or anger towards God. In an ugly mirror of the corporate world, expressing these feelings may be detrimental to the way you are perceived, and your promotional opportunities.

Failure to Lament

This failure to lament has a direct impact on our posture towards the poor—they are a physical theodicy that is best left out of sight in darkened alleyways, overseas slums and refugee camps. Sider seems to suggest that the failure of the Christian global north to be deeply troubled by social justice is an issue of biblical education:

> Most wealthy Christians have failed to seek God's perspective on the plight of our billion hungry neighbours... There are millions of Christians who will take any risk, make any sacrifice, forsake any treasure, if they clearly see that God's word demands it. (Sider 1997:40)

While I agree with Sider that a corrected understanding of Scripture would increase the average evangelical heart for the poor, I would argue it runs deeper than that. The global north perhaps does not need another Bible study as much as a lesson in how to shed an honest tear. Again, Brueggemann writes:

> A community of faith that negates lament soon concludes that the hard issues of justice are improper questions to pose at the throne [of God], because the throne seems to be only a place of praise. I believe it thus follows that if justice questions are improper questions at the throne... they soon appear to be improper questions in public places, in schools, in hospitals, with the government, and eventually even in the courts... we are left with only grim obedience and eventually despair. *The point of access for serious change has been forfeited when the propriety of this speech form is denied.* (1995a:107; emphasis mine)

Permitting only positive words in the context of a relationship with Yahweh results in and relies on an illusion that there is no injustice, that there is no poverty, there is no suffering—or at best, that Yahweh has nothing to say about these issues. In this setting, one must not just ignore the injustice, but the one who is enduring the injustice. It does not just forget the malnourished and swollen bellies of children; it overlooks the urgency that *they are children* and that there is something *terribly* wrong and unjust about malnourished children. It allows us to hear of terrible disasters and suffering without shedding a tear, and pray for those suffering without any stirrings of solidarity in our heart:

> "God, please be with the earthquake-affected folk in Nepal. Amen."

> "Next prayer point?"

I clearly remember a time when I believed that the poor somehow did not feel the pain of suffering as deeply as I did—until I began meeting people like the village leader in rural Sumba who had lost his wife and three children to cholera; until I attempted to treat the gangrenous legs of five-year-old Dexy and felt something of his mother's despair and helplessness; until I sat with a leper colony in Sabu and heard them express a quiet but deep pain at being isolated by their community.

These situations forced a choice upon me: Give up on the notion that the poor do not suffer, or give up on Yahweh who seemingly stands by while they suffer. It has been lament that offered a hand of fellowship and helped me hold this theodicean dilemma, while I attempt to sit with the poor in the presence of God. Failing to lament fosters a terrible, *terrible* disconnect between the Christian global north and our suffering family in the south. I am hopeful, however, that this can be readily undone if we take up this ancient tradition of our faith once again, making it a regular part of our life and worship.

Reconnecting Through Lament

Learning to lament, and using lament as a regular, spiritually formative practice will help integrate issues of social justice, both local and international, into the global north agenda (Brueggemann 1995a:106). Songs of lament strip away the false filters we build for ourselves, and "dangerously" help us to see the world as it really is (Brueggemann 1984:53).

As we open ourselves up entirely before God, warts and all, rational thoughts and irrational thoughts, with words of praise and lament, we become "liberated" towards both God and our neighbour (Gill 1989:119);

lament allows us, even forces us, to measure up our story against others, opening our eyes to our shared humanity (Broyles, 2008:386). It enables us to advocate for those who are suffering to the One who promised he would remove all suffering (Westermann 1981:276), while also forcing us to answer the same challenging questions: How have I contributed to the suffering? Why do I "stand far off" (Ps. 10)?

Lament builds solidarity between the global north and our suffering family in the south, and it also builds solidarity with Yahweh in declaring that the world is not as it should be. It causes us to be present to and understanding of suffering as Yahweh is (Hicks 1993:170), making us hungry for justice and mercy.

The regular use of lament can prepare the global north for times of disaster and news of disaster, as the process becomes embedded in our way of engaging with a broken and suffering world (Brueggemann 1984:67; Cohen 2013:75), while breaking down the false assumption that we know what God is doing in the world, forcibly reshaping our response to questions of theodicy. Perhaps one day a posture of embrace with silent tears of solidarity will replace the theologically-correct propositional statements and calls to repentance that Christians (myself included) have trotted out in times of suffering. I am convinced that the regular use of lament will assist us in this necessary transition.

LAMENT AND THE PRACTITIONER

The Impact of Working with the Poor

We turn now to consider the potential contribution of lament to the community development practitioner; for to be at the front end of poverty alleviation feeds questions of theodicy and issues of mental health. The very nature of development work is emotionally taxing, and many feel isolated and relatively unsupported; it is a common sentiment among community development practitioners that "there is nowhere to take the shit, but home" (Hoggett, Mayo, and Miller 2009:60).

It is a complex task involving the balancing of the many varied views of stakeholders, the impossibility of helping everyone and the evil of having to choose who will be assisted and who will be passed by. There is the constant dilemma of one's own wages and expenses coming out of project budgets meant to help the poor; the more I eat, the less they eat; the more I fly, the fewer we can help. It is no wonder that there are high rates of staff turnover in this sector; the mental burden can be significant (Hoggett et al. 2009:62).

Failure to Lament

Failing to deal with the distress and theological dilemmas associated with engaging poverty first-hand are the same for ignoring anguish and theodicy elsewhere: Practitioners can become "easily blindsided in particular situations and... involved in strange compensatory behaviours" (Ringma 2000:104).

This can only have a negative impact on the very situation we're seeking to address. Practitioners can become outcome oriented and rush or impose projects in hopes of belaying our fear of not making a difference, when the practitioner—to really make a difference—must in the first place have a posture of learning and be people oriented (Myers 1999:157; Chambers 1983:201).

This dilemma is particularly sharp for Christian practitioners raised in the environment of the Christian global north outlined above; practitioners who have had it drummed into them that Christ has triumphed over sin and that "there really are no other crises to be had" (Ringma 2000:108). We typically do not have a "theology of disasters" (Aten 2012:134). It is understandable then, as Melba Maggay posits:

> There is something about the daily exposure to poverty and other ills of society which tends to tear away faith and make agents of change some of the most cynical people around. (Myers 1999:163)

This runs the risk of agents of transformation ironically turning themselves into agents of destruction, where coping mechanisms such as violence, control, addiction and emotional withdrawal begin to take over as the formative characteristics of the practitioner. Being indefinitely angry at God has been demonstrated to result in mental and physical health deterioration (Snow et al. 2011:130), which is simply unsustainable for people who are working in an almost constant theodicean context.

The Potential Contribution of Lament

In dealing with the difficult task practitioners face, Chambers recommends taking time to reflect on others who have done great things (1983:216), Ife proposes reflective journaling (2013:305) and Myers suggests a mix of theological reflection, moderated expectation and detachment, among other things (1999:162f).

Myers' proposal comes closest to the process of lament—counselling and psychological help—and is a final option reserved for "critical incidents" (1999:166). While I greatly respect these authors and appreciate that Myers has even suggested spirituality as important to the practitioner, I believe their suggestions fall short of practitioners' needs.

My proposal is that lament offers Christian practitioners a way to be truly incarnational in approach, while holding the distress and "bringing the shit" to the One who sees the things they see and travels with them on the road, who will hear their hardest criticisms, weep with them, think no less of them for their despair, and gently remind them, when they are ready, that it is His problem to sort this mess out. Then, and *only* then, am I ready to hear an inspirational story, recite a popular fatalistic poem ("Lord, grant me the serenity...") and head back into the fray with a reckless and abandoned love.

It is shaking my fists at a loving Yahweh that allows me to slowly open my hands to embrace the disfigured and downtrodden. It is His listening to my despair that enables me to sit with the despairing. It is reflecting on His promises and character that reshapes *my* character and deepens my resolve and commitment to participating in the restoration of all things, in spite of the overwhelming task at hand. I identify more with Henri

Nouwen's Wounded Healer than Joel Osteen's You can, You will (2014). "I must bind my own wounds carefully, in anticipation of the moment when I will be needed... so that my wounds might be a major source of healing power" (Nouwen 2010:88f).

Perhaps that is too self-reflective, too much "I". But in the absence of research and qualitative studies in the area of lament for community development, I put myself forward as an example of a practitioner who has found and is finding lament to be a most helpful tool. While researching this paper, I penned a quick lament, to which the overwhelming response from those who read it was distress at my apparent distress. Ironically perhaps, the process was thoroughly cathartic for me:

> As I attempt a cheap plastic Band-Aid
> On the mountainous boil of the poor,
> I cry: "How long, O my God,
> Will you lie there—asleep, silent, snore?"
>
> Then I remember the ways
> You've acted in times past,
> And I glance again in their eyes,
> Seeing you, silently pleading with me,
> My question's U-turn realise.
>
> Your arms still embracing,
> Your hand on my shoulder,
> We start on the boil once more.
> I don't know how we'll do it,
> Or how, or when it'll end,
> But it's a Band-Aid I hear you ask for.

CONCLUSION

Lament has somehow been, for the most part, a tool left on the shelf of Christian antiquity—to be admired from a distance while it gathers dust.

It requires taking down and dusting off, for it is a breathing apparatus without which we will struggle to survive in the current climate. We need this important spiritual formation tool, and not just on the brightly lit, well-choreographed stages of modern Christian worship (although some chaos and despair would be helpful there too).

Lament has the ability to help strip away the Enlightenment-tinted glasses of the north, allowing us to serve and see the world as it really is. Lament can provide a healing framework for indigenous communities who suffer the theodicy of poverty in their very minds and bodies, and be a place of refuge and restoration for community development practitioners working in distressing situations.

There is an obsolescent nature to lament as it drives us closer to the day when "crying will be [needed] no more" (Rev. 24:1). I long for the day when lament will rightfully be a dust-gathering relic. Until then, however, I will continue to cry out to Yahweh, with the poor and—I hope—increasingly, the global north: "How long, O Lord?"

REFERENCES

Aten, J. D. 2012. "Disaster Spiritual and Emotional Care in Professional Psychology: A Christian Integrative Approach." *Journal of Psychology and Theology* 40(2):131–135.

Benner, D. G. 1990. *Healing Emotional Wounds*. Grand Rapids, MI: Baker Books.

Broyles, C. C. 2008. "Psalms of Lament." Pp. 384–398 in *Dictionary of the Old Testament; Wisdom, Poetry and Writings*, edited by Tremper Longman III and Peter Enns. Nottingham, UK: Inter-Varsity Press.

Brueggemann, W. 1984. *The Message of the Psalms: A Theological Commentary*. Minneapolis, MN: Augsburg Publishing.

------. 1995. *The Psalms and the Life of Faith*. Minneapolis, MN: Fortress Press.

Chambers, R. 1983. *Rural Development: Putting the Last First*. Essex, UK: Longman.

Cohen, D. J. 2013. *Why O Lord?* Milton Keynes, UK: Paternoster Press.

DeGroat, C. R. 2009. "The New Exodus: A Narrative Paradigm for Understanding Soul Care." *Journal of Psychology and Theology* 37(3):186–193.

Exline, J. J. and J. B. Grubbs. 2011. "'If I tell Others About My Anger Toward God, How Will They Respond?' Predictors, Associated Behaviours, and Outcomes in an Adult Example." *Journal of Psychology and Theology* 39(4):304–315.

Funk, M., N. Drew, M. Freeman, E. Faydi. 2010. Mental Health and Development. Geneva, Switzerland: World Health Organisation. Retrieved June 16, 2015 (http://whqlibdoc.who.int/publications/2010/9789241563949_eng.pdf?ua=1).

Gill, A. 1989. *Life on the Road: The Gospel Basis for a Messianic Lifestyle*. Homebush West, Australia: ANZEA Publishers.

Hankle, D. D. 2010. "The Therapeutic Implications of the Imprecatory Psalms in the Christian Counselling Setting." *Journal of Psychology and Theology* 38(4):275–280.

Hicks, R. 1993. *Failure to Scream*. Nashville, TN: Thomas Nelson.

Hoggett, P., M. Mayo, and C. Miller, 2009. *The Dilemmas of Development Work: Ethical Challenges in Regeneration*. Bristol, UK: The Policy Press.

Ife, J. and F. Tesoriero. 2006. *Community Development: Community-based Alternatives in an Age of Globalisation*. 3rd ed. Frenchs Forest, Australia: Pearson Education.

Ife, J. 2009. *Community Development in an Uncertain World: Vision, Analysis and Practice*. Melbourne, Australia: Cambridge University Press.

Konig, A., A. Eonta, and S. R. Dyal. 2014. "Enhancing the Benefits of Written Emotional Disclosure Through Response Training." *Behavior Therapy* 45(3):344–357.

Lasor, W. S., D. A. Hubbard, and F. W. Bush. 1996. *Old Testament Survey: The Message, Form and Background of the Old Testament. 2nd ed.* Grand Rapids, MI: William B. Eerdmans.

Lepore, S. J., P. Fernandez-Berrocal, J. Ragan, and N. Ramos. 2004. "It's Not That Bad: Social Challenges to Emotional Disclosure Enhance Adjustment to Stress." *Anxiety, Stress and Coping* 17(4):341–361.

Myers, B. L. 2000. *Walking With the Poor: Principles and Practices of Transformational Development*. Maryknoll, NY: Orbis Books.

Murali, V. and F. Oyebode 2004. "Poverty, Social Inequality and Mental Health." *Advances in Psychiatric Treatment* 10(3):216–224.

Nouwen, H. J. M. 2010. *The Wounded Healer. 2nd ed.* New York, NY: Crown Publishing.

Pennebaker, J. W. and S. K. Beall 1986. "Confronting a Traumatic Event: Towards an Understanding of Inhibition and Disease." *Journal of Abnormal Psychology* 96(3):274–281.

Ringma, C. R. 2000. *The Seeking Heart: A Journey with Henri Nouwen*. Brewster, MA: Paraclete Press.

Sider, R. J. 1997. *Rich Christians in an Age of Hunger: Moving from Affluence to Generosity. 4th ed.* Nashville, TN: W Publishing Group.

Snow, K. N., M. R. McMinn, R. K. Bufford, and I. A. Brendlinger. 2011. "Resolving Anger Toward God: Lament as an Avenue Toward Attachment." *Journal of Psychology and Theology* 39(2):130–142.

Stassen, G. H. and D. P. Gushee. 2003. *Kingdom Ethics: Following Jesus in Contemporary Context*. Downers Grove, IL: InterVarsity Press.

Summerton, R. and S. Wishart. 2004. "Casualties of War." Retrieved June 10, 2014 (https://www.youtube.com/watch?v=CZ505b1x2As).

Westen, D., L. Burton, and R. Kowalski. 2006. *Psychology*. Milton, Australia: John Wiley & Sons.

Westermann, C. 1981. *Praise and Lament in the Psalms*. Translated by Keith R. Crim and Richard N. Soulen. Atlanta, GA: John Knox Press.

Worden, J. W. 2001. *Grief Counselling and Grief Therapy. 3rd ed.* East Sussex, UK: Brunner-Routledge.

Spiritual Formation, Leadership & Kingdom Ministry

Margaret Loy Choon Ming

Christian ministry is challenging in the 21st century in the midst of postmodern thinking, mega churches, mega ministries, mega Christian concerts and popular Christian music groups, declining missions and growing religious polarisations, and extremism. Many Christians involved in ministry are expected to be more, know more, give more, and do more in an increasingly complex society and work organisational structure. Fast-paced, multitasking ministries often take their toll.

Many believers desire to serve the Lord ardently, and often do so passionately when they first become Christians. However, over time, we begin to see some who will persevere and continue to grow in faithful service, while others who falter in serving or drop out of active service but still attend church. This research is based on ten respondents, six of whom are Malaysians, and four of whom are expatriates who have continued serving in various capacities through their ups and downs over more than 20 years each.

The original research on which this chapter is based sought to examine three interrelated questions:

- What makes the first group persevere in their ministry and remain faithful in their vocational calling?
- How did they handle the challenges that came their way, and how do they now understand their faith journey?
- What place do theology and spiritual disciplines play in their spiritual formation and faithful ministry?

These research questions enable us to explore the connections between theology, spiritual formation, leadership, and faithful holistic ministry.

LITERATURE REVIEW

A quick review of the literature on spiritual formation will set the context before examining the life journeys of the ten respondents. Their responses were analysed within a spiritual formation framework to see what enabled them to persevere in faithful ministry, be it their understanding of theology, their spiritual formation, their leadership journeys, or the outworking of their ministry.

What is Spiritual Formation?

Willard contends that "Spiritual formation is about agape love, how much it has captured a Christian's heart and changed them, for the heart is where freedom exists and choices determined". He argues that spiritual formation involves the body, "because that's where we live and what we live from... resulting in *transformation of the whole person*, including the body in its social context. Spiritual formation is never merely inward" (emphasis mine; Willard, n.d.:5, 7).

Parker Palmer speaks of the *integration of action-and-contemplation*, where action is any way in which we "co-create reality with other beings and with the Spirit", and contemplation as "any way that we can unveil the illusions that masquerade as reality and reveal the reality behind the masks" (1990:17). Palmer also challenges us to maintain an attitude of *abundance instead of scarcity*, and an *eternal versus present horizon* as we act in faith, so that the active life of work, creativity and caring can *take us towards the fullness of new life* for ourselves and the whole of creation (Ibid:152–157).

Taylor distinguishes two kinds of prayer: The prayer of movement, "where [a person's] mind moves from thought to thought and from image to image", versus the prayer of stillness, where "the mind stands still and looks, takes in what is standing before it and gives itself" (1972:236). The first is commonly known as meditation, and the second, contemplation. Contemplation is a skill we need to relearn, to deal with "the unceasing movement of our conscious minds, combined with the strain and noise" we live in (Ibid: 239).

Spiritual formation for Henri Nouwen is the integration of the three themes of "solitude, community and compassion". In one of his latest books, produced posthumously by two of his students, he explains how all three themes integrate together:

> The Word of God is first of all read in community, silence is first a part of our life together, spiritual direction first needs to be seen and experienced as direction in the name of the larger community, and ministry is a vocation given by and performed in the name of the community of faith. Thus Spiritual Formation means ongoing formation of the *heart* (emphasis mine), in community life, expressed in service to the world."[1] (Nouwen, Christensen, and Laird, 2010:xxviii)

Jeffrey Greenman, President and Professor of Theology and Ethics at Regent College in Canada, gives another definition of spiritual formation

---

[1] Nouwen's teachings were compiled into three posthumous volumes, *Spiritual Formation*, *Spiritual Direction* and *Spiritual Discernment*, by two of his long-time students, Michael Christensen and Rebecca Laird.

that emphasises responding to God's grace, Christlikeness, and the work of the Holy Spirit.

> Spiritual formation is our continuing response to the reality of God's grace shaping us into the likeness of Jesus Christ, through the work of the Holy Spirit, in the community of faith, for the sake of the world. (Greenman, 2010:24)

I concur with Greenman that "spiritual formation at its best involves a reciprocal dynamic between gathering and scattering, contemplation and action, silence and speech, being and doing, receiving and giving" (Ibid: 27). In fact, the inward and outward journeys provide impetus for one another. As we know God better, we identify with his heart and his mission more and more. As we see the brokenness in the world, we turn to God for his wisdom, grace, and strength, without which we cannot even begin to minister his unconditional love. Greenman, Nouwen and Palmer all emphasise this reciprocal dynamic of the inward and outward journeys.

The three classical prayer practices for intimacy with God are the *prayer of examen*, *lectio divina*, and *centring prayer* (Campolo and Darling, 2013:91). The first is more reflective at the end of each day and helps us move from self-awareness to God-awareness (Ibid:92). *Lectio divina* enables us to pray the scriptures in order to know God's heart and be Jesus' "friend" through the work of the Holy Spirit (Ibid:91). Centring prayer helps us to deepen our intimacy with God in contemplation, in stillness with God (Ibid:131, 133).

Benner's description of lectio divina as movements of a dance led by the Spirit is helpful, as it gives me the liberty to behold God with my whole being and not just to read God's Word analytically and systematically (2010:53–56). A dance can be beautiful only when one experiences it as a whole, when one follows the lead of another, not when both try to lead, or when one is uncooperative. Benner's goal is to help readers discover a life of transformational prayer which goes beyond times of prayer into lives that are in communion with God.

Spiritual Development Theories

Several spiritual development theories provide guidance for our exploration. Another multidimensional framework for our own assessment and understanding will be proposed, to enable growth and longevity in faithful ministry.

Robert Clinton and Leadership Maturity

Clinton (2006) believes that leaders mature along a "generalized timeline with 5 to 6 development phases".

Phase 1	Phase 2	Phase 3	Phase 4	Phase 5	Phase 6
Sovereign Foundation	Inner-Life Growth	Ministry Maturing	Life Maturing	Convergence	Afterglow

Figure 1: The Generalised Timeline (Clinton, 2006:44)

He sees Phase 1 as personality and character traits and life experiences which, in time, can be used by God as building blocks. Phase 2 is when an emerging leader is formed primarily inwards, with both formal and informal training. Clinton acknowledges that in real life, Phases 3 to 5 often overlap, though he shows them in sequential phases (2006:30–31). Only sometimes will there be a Phase 6, Afterglow, where the fruit of a lifetime of ministry and growth culminates in an era of recognition or influence at broad levels (Ibid:47).

For Clinton, ministry fruitfulness is *not* the focus in Phases 1to 3, as God is working *in* the emerging leader, not *through* the person. By Phase 4, a mature fruitfulness is the result, and "isolation, crisis and, conflict take on new meaning". This is when the leader's character matures and mellows, and ministry flows out of being. In Phase 5, "God moves the leader into a role that matches his/her gift mix and experience so that ministry is maximized" (Ibid:45–46). A leader's response to God's guidance at the *Convergence* phase is to "trust, rest and watch".

Peter Scazzero and Emotionally Healthy Spirituality

Peter Scazzero subscribes generally to the idea of spiritual development in seasons, and that there will be a time when a Christian will hit "the Wall" and then seek the inward journey, or vice versa, where the journey inward had led them, through the wall. Either way, the journey outward is then from a more centred place, with God continuously allowing more events and people into our lives to transform us.

"For most of us, the Wall appears through a crisis that turns our world upside down" (Scazzero, 2006:120). He believes that the Wall may appear in various ways throughout our lifetimes (Ibid:121) and we may get stuck there (Ibid:122). The Wall is Scazzero's metaphor for the 'Dark Night of the Soul'.

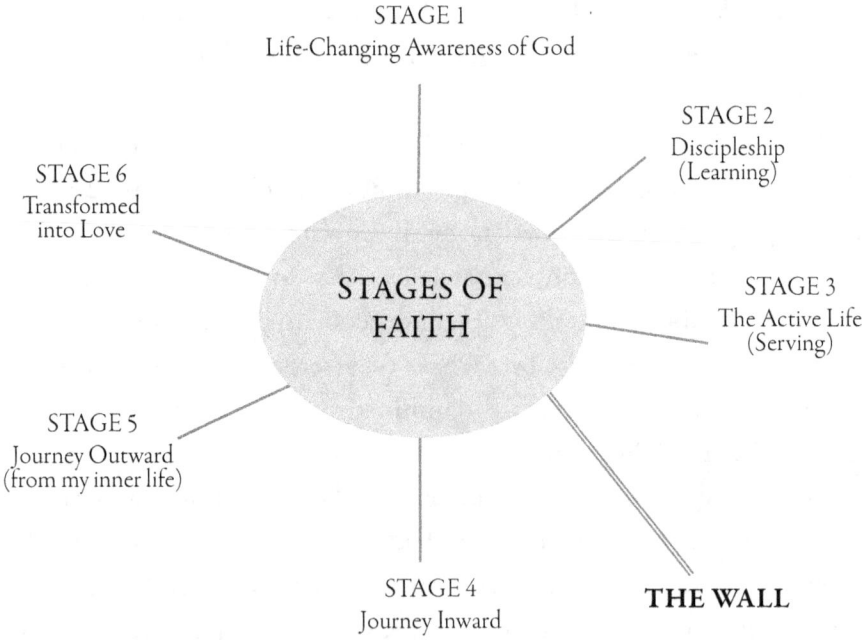

STAGE 1
Life-Changing Awareness of God

STAGE 2
Discipleship
(Learning)

STAGE 6
Transformed
into Love

STAGES OF
FAITH

STAGE 3
The Active Life
(Serving)

STAGE 5
Journey Outward
(from my inner life)

STAGE 4
Journey Inward

THE WALL

Figure 2: Stages in a Life of Faith (Scazzero, 2006:119)

Scazzero believes that the combination of emotional health and contemplative spirituality can fill the gap in contemporary Christianity and together, they unleash the Holy Spirit inside us to know experientially the power of an authentic life in Christ (Ibid:46). He and his wife, Geri, teach how to deal with the dark sides of ourselves using "Emotionally Healthy Skills" (his second video series), which used to be taught to counsellors. Having worked through the skills, I can testify that they are indeed helpful in learning about ourselves and relating better to each other to bring out our authentic selves.

Nouwen's Spiritual Development Theory

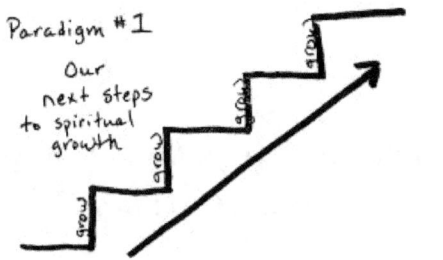

Paradigm 1: Classical Spiritual Development Theory – Steps or Stages of growth

Paradigm 2: Nouwen's Spiritual Development Theory

Figure 3: Comparison of Classical vs. Nouwen's Spiritual Development Theory (Edwards, 2015)

The movement of the Spirit... tends to come in cycles throughout our lives, with only a broad and hardly predictable progressive order. Instead of stepping up to higher and higher stages, as if achieving one stage leads to the next level and the next, we tend to vacillate back and forth between the poles that we seek to resolve. We move "from fear to love" and then back "from love to fear," for example in a dynamic process that is never complete. Rather than resolving the tensions once and for all, the movements continue to call us to conversion and transformation. Rather than allowing us to conquer some aspect of life and move on to the next stage of spiritual development, we are called to return to prayer, to love, and to intimacy with God. (Nouwen et al., 2010:135)

Though the tensions and the movements mentioned by both Benner and Nouwen are understandable, the data from the ten respondents may suggest another way to understand the integrated spiritual development of a Christian in ministry. This proposed model will have elements similar to the five-fold dimensions of spiritual formation as examined above, with the added work of Scazzero's understanding of Emotionally Healthy Spirituality. This framework is dynamic and can help individuals reflect on where they are and commit to work on different areas as they move forward in their journeys.

WHAT ENABLES BELIEVERS TO PERSEVERE IN MINISTRY AND REMAIN FAITHFUL TO THEIR VOCATIONAL CALLING?

Search Institute developed an educational tool with a list of 40 developmental assets which enable young people to develop into successful and contributing adults. The less internal assets they have, the more they need to depend on their external assets. Both internal and external assets are needed for a young person to be successful.[2] The external assets require the cooperation of others, such as family members and teachers, for support.

Similarly, after analysing the respondents' feedbacks in the light of the literature reviewed, the following frameworks seem to emerge. Figure 4 shows the Holy Spirit at work in a believer's life (the spokes of the circle), renewing the mind (theology), transforming and centring the heart, changing character, producing emotional maturity, drawing people in inclusive community, and empowering the person for obedience to the Kingdom Mission, as the Christian responds to God's grace and love.

---

[2] See "Developmental Assets" (http://www.search-institute.org/our-research/developmental-assets). An example of the 40 Developmental Assets required by adolescents are available for reference   (http://www.search-institute.org/content/40-developmental-assets-adolescents-ages-12-18).

These are the processes at work in different areas and different seasons of the person's life. The six processes overlap and feed into one another and cannot be easily separated in life, but are analysed as different segments for the purposes of clarity for this paper.

These dynamic processes involve the heart, the mind, the emotions , and the will in the respondents' relationship with God, their community of faith, and their wider ministry community. The fruits of their lives and ministries are visible and bear witness to their spirituality.

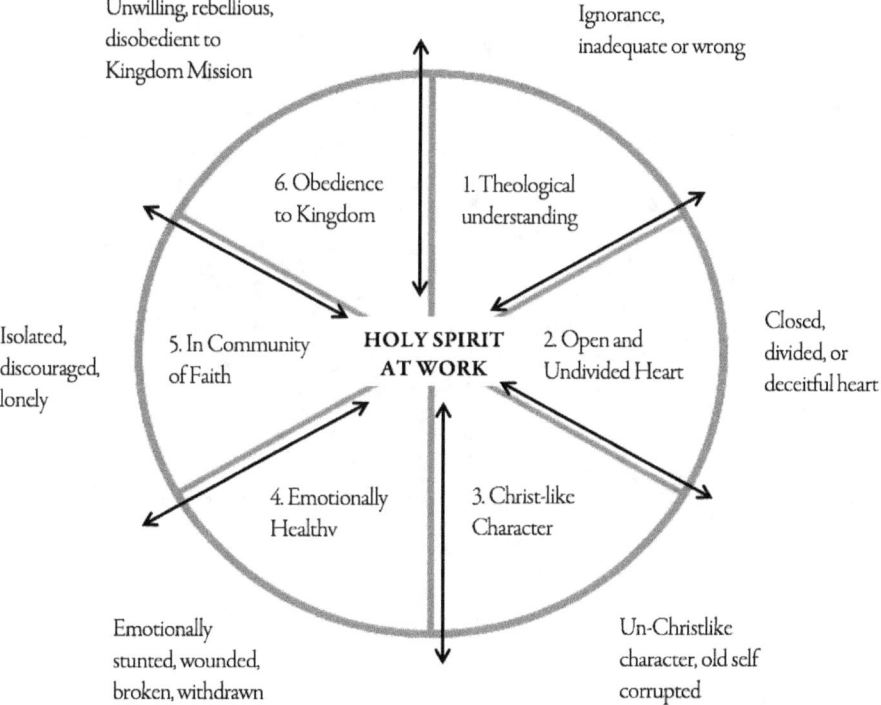

Figure 4: Work of the Holy Spirit in a Christian's life in Spiritual Transformation as the Christian responds to God's grace and love in Spiritual Formation.

Each segment (area) can grow and shrink at different times and in different seasons if we do not guard our hearts and reflectively respond to God's Spirit in our being and doing. The world, the flesh and the Evil One continue to be at work in our lives and the world. However, our confidence is in the Lord, for he has overcome the Evil One. He has also empowered us to stand against the flesh and the world by His Spirit. Each area of our lives supports the other and, when held in tension, enables us to be integrated in our contemplation-and-action.

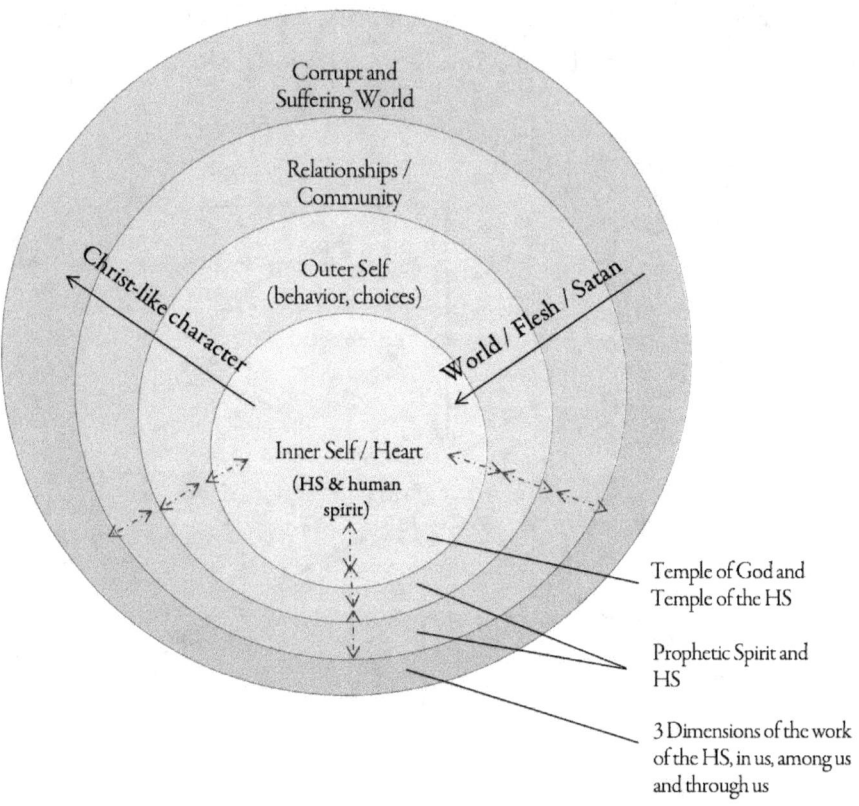

Figure 5: A Christian's spiritual formation impacting the person's outer self, relationships, community and the world (modified from Averbeck, 2008).

Figure 5 shows the inside-out movement, and the three-dimensional of the work of the Spirit in us, among us and through us as we resist the world, the flesh and the Evil One, which seek to corrupt and destroy us. Paul spoke to the Ephesian Christians at length in Ephesians 4:20–32 about their own personal and corporate sanctification. He reminded them "to put off your old self, which is being corrupted by its deceitful desires; to be made new in the attitude of your minds; and to put on the new self, created to be like God in true righteousness and holiness" (Ephesians 4:22b–24).

Findings and Analysis with Reference to Figures 4 and 5

The respondents who embraced their ministry more singularly and lived more joyfully had greater theological understanding of integral mission and did not dichotomise between who they are and what they do. Some of their contexts had changed from vocational Christian ministry to outside the institutional church. Two-thirds of the respondents credit their theological understanding and desire to see lives transformed for shaping their involvement in ministry.

All of the respondents mentioned cultivating the presence of God through prayer, contemplation, and/or study. Most maintain a regular devotional reading of the Bible and practise times of reflection and solitude to intentionally maintain their openness to God. All the respondents went through different crises and times of weariness in their lives. Most also experienced disappointment, brokenness and hurt in ministry. More than half the respondents had to work through conflicts and personal or family illnesses. Many shared that they journeyed through these in lonely circumstances, with some in difficult ministry situations, including being in conflict zones. Almost half described their times as experiencing the shadow of death. Some described losing hope, facing depression, experiencing personal failures, nearing burnout, being lost, and almost being at the edge. Many of them felt their time with God had become routine and dry. Others withdrew from ministry temporarily, some took sabbaticals, and some left their contexts of ministry.

In mapping their restoration, the vast majority found personal learning and participating in spiritual retreats helpful. They changed their way and pace of life, learned and practised new life-giving spiritual disciplines, took more intentional Sabbath rests, read more, sought more spiritual and psychological insights, and worked more with the vulnerable in society.

More than half spoke of being more discerning of the Holy Spirit. Less than half developed relationships with mentors or had the privilege of pastoral or member care.

Half of the respondents spoke of embracing pain and mourning their loss and hurts. An overlapping half spoke of allowing the Lord to love, restore, and heal them. Another half spoke of surrendering the past to God. A few experienced being pursued by the Father's love. Others reprioritised and focused on the essentials in their lives. None of the respondents had become bitter, but most had become more reflective of their lives' journeys, while not minimising their own faults or the faults of others or the organisations they were with. Most recalled the posture of their hearts to be trusting of God, though some were angry, broken-hearted, and felt disconnected.

Two-thirds of the respondents spoke of how their perspectives had changed through their pain and trials. Half spoke of being humbled and becoming more understanding. They would not judge so readily and would weigh matters more carefully. They felt more empathy for the weak and struggling. A few spoke of being more secure of their identity in Christ and nearly half have become more open and willing to be vulnerable. Their character had been moulded.

In terms of emotional health, all the respondents had embraced their past conflicts and pain and were more thankful. The majority had also adopted different rhythms of life. However, only half had established clear boundaries and paced their ministry demands. Almost all found that supportive friends were most helpful in their personal and ministry journey. More than half shared that they find mutual encouragement through ministry peers and those they are discipling as well. Less than half depended on counselling and spiritual friends. Only one of the respondents lived in a Catholic community with other brothers. The married couples found support in their spouses.

Out of the respondents' trials and difficulties, their Christlike characters were forged. This can be seen in their different responses to life and ministry in the ensuing years, where many chose to minister out of the limelight, outside denominational hierarchy and position, and contribute in quiet ways in the kingdom of God. Some of them do so at great cost to themselves and their families. Most chose to live in simplicity and service. Their thankfulness translates into generosity and submission to Christ. A few respondents mentioned that their intentional choice of working alongside the vulnerable, though difficult, was highly fulfilling as they obeyed God. In doing this, they chose to keep their relationship with God paramount and not allow past hurts, position or acclaim to divert them.

Many of the respondents were serving in unconventional areas of ministry at the time of the interviews, such as community services and/or development, cross-cultural missions, spiritual formation, theological research and writing, advocacy, and creative ministry. The majority of the respondents had engaged in ministry with the vulnerable, including those with disabilities, indigenous peoples, foreigners, migrants, refugees, the poor, young people and children at risk, the marginalised, trafficking victims, and the oppressed. Knowing God's heart compelled the respondents to act in solidarity with and on behalf of those suffering as a result of various injustices.

REFLECTIONS BASED ON ANALYSIS

Many of us who try to spend time with God know the difficulties of entering into prayer and intimacy with God. We are encouraged to press on, despite our wounded-ness, activism, distrust and inner darkness. In fact, Houston says that

> Encountering darkness in our lives should not drive us from prayer, *but drive us to prayer*. Darkness only becomes an obstacle when we fail to see God as the powerful ruler of our lives, able to overcome the evil we face in spite of our fears and feelings. (Houston, 1989:51)

During their times of difficulties, some respondents went through a period of withdrawal from people and Christian programmes, and spent time in retreats and nurturing their personal and family lives. They had to attend to the demands of their own hearts, which they seemed to have put aside due to the demands of ministry.

> When the Father begins crafting character, a crushing must first take place, not because He's a temperamental artist who's angry with His work, but because the raw materials for His art come from a broken heart. (Gire, 1998)

Those who confronted their past hurts and acknowledged their helplessness with the assistance of skilled counsellors and mentors, or had a close friend or spouse journeying with them, coped better and emerged sooner. Healing of their emotions and a return to emotional health seemed to take longer, as most Christian traditions have not made emotional health or well-being an emphasis and often lack the perspective that it is an important area to work on.

> Job focused on the Author of Life in the midst of his intense suffering and pain. He was authentic with God, had sincere dialogue with him, both speaking and listening (Fiorello, 2011:184).

When we encounter Christ in our prayer, we have to come to the end of ourselves and be shattered of our own personalities, accomplishments and acclaim. We need to be unmasked to come face to face with Him (Houston, 1989:63). Until we deeply understand our true emptiness and insufficiency, we cannot hunger and thirst for God and his righteousness and long for his sufficiency. Prayer expresses our relationship with God (Houston, 1989:54). It gives us coherence in a broken world and overcomes our own fragmentation inside. It can bring healing to our divided selves and to our divided relationships with other people (Ibid:56–57)

The feedback of the respondents attests to the importance and truth of the reciprocal dynamic of the inward and outward journeys in spiritual formation. It seems that the more profound the respondents' relationship with God, the more it becomes expressed in outward ministry to the vulnerable, and the more "natural" such ministry feels to the respondents.

Most of the respondents lived with the eternal in perspective as they chose to move out of their comfort zone to minister in their unique areas of God's calling. Most respondents shared that they grew in their walk with God as they obeyed Him. It seemed to be their constant learning and wrestling before God that kept their relationship with Him fresh, and kept the respondents journeying with their Saviour and Lord.

Even when we find it hard to pray, "Christ prays for [us]"! (Dawn, 2006:74) Marva Dawn told the story of a conversation with Eugene Peterson regarding her own prayer struggles, and he told her to stop trying so hard! Marva was reminded that "the Trinity who continually creates us, redeems us, and empowers us also cares intimately for our health and wholeness, for our wellness as servants of the Church and the world... and a confident awareness that each of us is God's beloved!" (Ibid:75)

In contrast, most of the respondents felt disappointed and some even angry with a large part of the institutional church that had "compartmentalised spirituality and social justice". They lamented their lonely journeys as they perceived the church to be complacent and not having a counter-cultural witness. A few respondents were pained to see hypocrisy and politics in Christian institutions, with some leaders using coercive means to grow their congregations. Some found the local churches had a localised ecclesiology, but lacked a global, outward, and more kingdom focus.

Old Testament professor John Goldingay shows that Israel's spirituality was expressed in its values, decision, and ethics (Goldingay, 2009:585). It was observed in their character, that is, their commitment, love, compassion, patience, peace-ableness, forgiveness and care for others, even their enemies (Ibid:590–595). It was observed in their disgust and anger at sin, and in the integrity and wholeness of their lives. Israel walked in integrity of heart, mind, and action. It was called to holiness and purity. Its visible holiness and practices were distinctive. However, we know also that Israel did not *continue* in holiness; its failure resulted in God's judgment against it.

Averbeck gives a corporate view of spiritual formation. He sees it as "the work of the Holy Spirit in the human spirit forming and shaping [lives] from the inside out... building the local communities of faith... [to become] the prophetic communities through whom the world hears the gospel and sees its transforming effects" (Averbeck, 2008:53). He showed how spiritual formation relates finally to Christians becoming prophetic communities whose corporate presence is their witness. All the respondents longed to be part of this kind of distinctive and prophetic community.

There seemed to be some correlation between theological training and faithful ministry. However, the *level* of formal theological training did not necessarily make any difference in the degree of intimacy indicated by the respondents. Instead, it is the *nature* of the training that seemed to have enabled many of the respondents to experience greater intimacy with him. The spiritual intimacy and journeys of the respondents were more crucial, irrespective of theological education or training. Theological training and intentional spiritual formation seemed to help respondents to articulate and frame their thinking and experiences. Others who are still faithful in ministry, who had missionary and theological training but did not seem to have been exposed to spiritual formation earlier, seemed to have struggled more in ministry.

PERSONAL REFLECTIONS

Church history is full of examples of how the saints' "love for Christ, intensified through their commitment to spiritual practices, produced in [them] intense desires to share Christ and help the poor and oppressed" (Campolo and Darling, 2013:91). I was moved most by four of the respondents, three of whom are male and one female.

The two male respondents were more mature and had worked through their theology and determined their values and priorities earlier in life. Though one is married and the other was not (and has since gone to the Lord), they ministered out of the security of their identity in Christ, knowing God's heart for people and for justice. One had a ministry in assisting others in spiritual formation, while another is an advocate for sound theology, religious freedom, human rights, and justice. The single male respondent lived in a Catholic community with other Catholic brothers and he found their corporate life together enriching. The married male respondent ploughed on, though the going is tough, and not many share in his passion of bearing sound intellectual witness in multicultural Malaysia.

The third male respondent is married but younger. He walked away from his ministry appointment and went into itinerant ministry with little fixed income when he saw in his own heart that his position had begun to mean more to him than people or the Lord. His spirituality allowed him to see the deceitfulness in his own heart, and his security in Christ gave him the courage to walk away from financial security and give up the need for recognition. One female respondent stood out as she had confronted her sexual brokenness in the past and had come to a place of restfulness. She is now in a ministry helping others who are marginalised through their gender confusion and sexual brokenness.

The three respondents reached life convergence where their spirituality, values, skills, and knowledge enable them to minister freely out of their beings. They have been able to integrate their contemplation and action, and the Holy Spirit has worked in them from the inside out to impact their worlds.

Spiritual formation is also radical attachment, a "rootedness" to a crucified Christ. Augsburger cites Moltmann, who points out that a radical commitment to Jesus in our Christian faith requires the "pain of repentance and fundamental change", and pits a person against oneself and one's environment, making one "rootless" and "homeless" to follow Christ. This "religion of the cross" usually scandalises our co-religionists instead of harmonising us with them! (Augsburger, 2006:26)

Authentic discipleship is thus "three dimensional, a life of self-transforming, God encountering, and other embracing" (Ibid:26–27). It is thus a spirituality of self-surrender, love of God and love of neighbour, which is evident in the disciple's actions and practice.

A radical attachment calls us to be attuned to Jesus, to imitate the Jesus of the Gospels, the Jesus of the Sermon on the Mount, who calls us to leave all and to follow Him. The outworking of our faith is found in doing His work in His way, "in self-forgetful honouring of his name" (Ibid:53). The majority of the respondents exhibited this radical commitment to Christ.

A few respondents continue to serve faithfully despite experiencing dissonance in not being able to fully integrate their spirituality, values and personal ministry as their organisation, church or supporters did not fully embrace their values and vision. Yet, they are doing what they can in their contexts. This is a reminder and an encouragement too as we persevere in hope. The church is called to a posture of patience and of intercession.

We are living in the 'now' and the 'not yet' (1 John 3:2, Heb. 2:9). All the respondents shared a generosity in spirit as they chose to give their time and effort to be part of this research. Many, in the midst of their simplicity of lifestyle, live from a place of abundance and not scarcity.

CONCLUSION

> Being formed in the image of Christ integrates believers into God's mission for the redemption of all creation, not simply as a specific role in a particular mission, but as a life hid with Christ in God, that incarnates God's redemptive activity in the midst of the world as it is. Indeed, spiritual formation in Christ and mission with Christ are inseparable components in our participation in God's redemption of all creation. (Mulholland, 2013:17)

Spiritual formation is an integral part of leadership formation. The key finding seemed to be not so much about how the respondents had remained faithful in ministry, but how they have grown in their Christian maturity, in their inner capacity.

Their growth included growth in Christian spirituality, Christlike character, emotional health and kingdom mission through their brokenness and life experiences, and through the empowering of the Holy Spirit.

Formal theological equipping, intentional spiritual formation, reflections, debriefing and interventions, and spiritual friendships enriched and enlarged their capacity. Kingdom ministry and life experiences became both the crucible of their formation as well as the outworking of their faith.

The respondents also reflected on their experience of God's love and grace throughout their journeys, with many of them being very thankful for their experiences and the opportunity to grow as well as to serve his kingdom purposes now. Their inner growth resulted in a greater graciousness and humility in the way they relate to fellow believers and the world. They minister with a greater restfulness, though some still do so in challenging and lonely situations. Their longing and desire seem to be for more spiritual community, and for the institutional church to rise to its kingdom role of being a missional witness instead of being so much part of the world.

The research also showed that there are still people who are quietly and gently bearing kingdom witness for Christ, as they still keep in communion with our Trinitarian God. Though this research focused mostly on people who started in formal ministry, yet the findings may be applicable for all Christians in the ordinary messiness of our lives. Jacob's story shows us that God pursues and transforms people in the very ordinary, even boring stuff of life. (R. Paul Stevens, 2013:182–183)

It was humbling to have had the privilege to speak with the different respondents about their personal and ministry journeys. What they revealed about their inner world are their gifts to us, for our mutual learning and edification.

The greatest gap revealed by this limited research is the lack of missional communities for these respondents to be part of. Therefore, there is an urgent need to cultivate spiritual friendships and be intentional in finding and belonging to a missional team ministry, instead of doing ministry alone. There is also a need to focus on the emotional health and well-being of those in ministry, and an intentional community can be part of the solution.

Thus, the institutional church needs to take these findings seriously. Christian spirituality is to be socially engaged (Gushee, 2010:213). Christian ethics and human suffering should concern Christians as human beings are created, sustained, and redeemed by God in Christ (Ibid:214). Hence, it should form our convictions and practice, causing us to have an "ethic of life" (Ibid:216). This should then govern our stand on public issues such as abortion, the death penalty, human-induced climate change ,and the demonisation of gays and lesbians.

Charles Elliott showed us that praying the kingdom together is needful, but we cannot assume that we know the shape of the kingdom (Elliott, 1985:22) or that it is synonymous with certain political changes or political parties (Ibid:26–27). He encourages us to "move towards [the poor/suffering]" with a greater degree of "empathy, of friendliness, of readiness to share, that would culminate in real welcome, actual standing alongside" (Ibid:29). It is an increasing awareness, an attunement in our state of consciousness that we can stand with the poor. "The call to prayer for the Kingdom is a call to be acquainted with the poor and marginalized in our own community" (Ibid:29).

The Holy Spirit continues the work of Christ in us. He is not only in us individually, but also corporately. He also shapes us into a missional community. The Holy Spirit draws our attention to Jesus Christ, towards greater complexity and sensitiveness, to realise our personhood. He alone opens our inward eye both individually and corporately to see the sovereignty of the risen Christ (Taylor, 1972:108). The question then for the Church is how we cultivate this sensitivity to the Holy Spirit corporately.

Lastly, for all those like the respondents who have radically followed Christ and embraced the call of the kingdom of God, Melba Maggay reminds us to guard our inner life as "daily exposure to poverty and other ills... wears away faith and makes agents of change some of the most cynical people around". She reminds us of Ecclesiastes 7:16, to not be "over-righteous" nor "over-wise". Maggay advocates the postures of brokenness, faith, detachment, rest, obedience, discernment, and waiting.[3] These can only be attained in God's presence and not our own strength (1996:81–92).

May God continue to be our individual and corporate source of grace, hope, and strength!

---

[3]   In the long fight for societal transformation, Melba Maggay exhorts Christians to:
- Learn "how to fail—how to learn our lessons from the experience of defeat and pick ourselves up again and start anew" (2 Cor. 4:8–10).
- Put on the "whole armour of God", especially "the shield of faith" (Eph. 6:13–17).
- Practise a certain amount of detachment—to practise the Sabbath and rest, so that the ministry does not become an idol.
- Recognise that "social transformation requires a long obedience,... consciously develop endurance, the ability to outlast the opposition and prevail in the long war of attrition" (Prov. 24:10, Jer. 12:5).
- "Conserve energy" and "be selective about our fights", recognising the season and timing of God.
- Recognise that "ultimately transforming society is really the work of God", and wait in hope.

REFERENCES

Augsburger, David. 2006. *Dissident Discipleship: A Spirituality of Self-Surrender, Love of God, and Love of Neighbor.* Grand Rapids, MI: Brazos Press.

Averbeck, Richard E. 2008. "Spirit, Community, and Mission: A Biblical Theology for Spiritual Formation." *Journal of Spiritual Formation & Soul Care 1*(1):27–53.

Benner, David G. 2010. *Opening to God.* Downers Grove, IL: InterVarsity Press.

Clinton, J. Robert 2006. *The Making of a Leader.* Colorado Springs, CO: NavPress.

Campolo, Tony and Mary A. Darling. 2013. *The God of Intimacy and Action.* London: SPCK.

Dawn, Marva J. 2006. *The Sense of the Call.* Grand Rapids, MI: Eeardmans.

Edwards, Pam. 2015. "Adults Want Help With Spiritual Growth… What's Your Next Step?" VantagePoint3. Retrieved June 19, 2015 (http://vantagepoint3.org/adults-want-help-with-spiritual-growth-whats-your-next-step).

Elliott, Charles. 1985. *Praying the Kingdom: Towards a Political Spirituality.* London: Darton, Longman & Todd.

Fiorello, Michael D. 2011. "Aspects of Intimacy with God in the Book of Job." *Journal of Spiritual Formation & Soul Care* 4(2):155–184.

Gire, Ken Jr. 1998. *Moments With the Saviour.* Grand Rapids, MI: Zondervan.

Goldingay, John. 2009. *Old Testament Theology, vol. 3, Israel's Life.* Downers Grove,IL: InterVarsity Press.

Greenman, Jeffrey P. 2010. "Spiritual Formation in Theological Perspective." Pp. 23–25 in *Life in the Spirit: Spiritual Formation in Theological Perspective*, edited by Jeffrey P. Greenman and George Kalantzis. Downers Grove, IL: InterVarsity Press.

Gushee, David. 2010. "Spiritual Formation and the Sanctity of Life." Pp. 213–228 in *Life in the Spirit: Spiritual Formation in Theological Perspective*, edited by Jeffrey P. Greenman and George Kalantzis. Downers Grove, IL: InterVarsity Press.

Houston, James. 1989. *Prayer the Transforming Friendship.* Oxford, UK: Lion.

Maggay, Melba. 2011. *Transforming Society.* Eugene, OR: Wipf and Stock Publishers.

Mulholland, Robert M. 2013. "Spiritual Formation in Christ and Mission with Christ." *Journal of Spiritual Formation & Soul Care* 6(1):11–17.

Nouwen, Henri J. M., Christensen Michael J., and Rebecca J. Laird. 2010. *Spiritual Formation: Following the Movements of the Spirit.* New York, NY: Harper One.

Palmer, Parker J. 1990. *The Active Life: A Spirituality of Work, Creativity and Caring.* San Francisco, CA: Jossey-Bass.

Scazzero, Peter. 2006. *Emotionally Healthy Spirituality.* Nashville, TN: Thomas Nelson.

Stevens, R. Paul. 2013. *Down-to-earth Spirituality.* Downers Grove, IL: InterVarsity Press.

Taylor, John V. 1972. *The Go-between God: The Holy Spirit and Christian Mission.* London: SCM Press.

Willard, Dallas. N.d. "Spiritual Formation: What it is, and How it is Done." Retrieved from http://www.dwillard.org/articles/individual/spiritual-formation-what-what-it-is-and-how-it-is-done.

DVD: Dallas Willard lecture: Taking Theology & Spiritual Discipline into the Marketplace, Retrieved September 16, 2011 (http://open.biola.edu/resources/taking-theology-and-spiritual-discipline-into-the-marketplace).

Contemplation and Action: An Exploration of a Symbiotic Relationship

Lee Soo Choo

Four years ago, at the end of two decades of almost non-stop active ministry, a friend asked what I would be doing next. I replied that I would like to sleep for a year! My frantic life of 'doings' had left me exhausted, hollow and wanting. Work should not be wearisome, I thought. I longed for rest, for stillness, for a divine centeredness. That started me on a profoundly important journey, a quest for inner integration and wholeness. I came to realise that spiritual formation in Christ is not optional but an integral part of doing the mission of God.

Christian spiritual formation, according to Henri Nouwen, is a "process of self-emptying and spirit-filling—the gradual development of the heart of God in the life of a human being, aided by contemplative prayer, inclusive community, and compassionate ministry" (2011a:5). This process is likened to an inward search (of self and God) or journey within; what others call the interior life, the inner life, or *contemplation*. The expression outwards to community and ministry, or outward journey, is commonly referred to as the outer life, the active life, or simply, *action*.

There is an assumed (and sometimes disastrous) dichotomy between this inner and outer formation, between action and contemplation, between Christian spirituality and mission. Hence this essay will explore the symbiotic relationship between action and contemplation, the journeys inward, upward, and outward, and how they can be integrated. It is important to note that what follows are not the reflections of a disinterested observer. Rather, they emerge out of the experience of one who is learning the deep need to bring action and contemplation into a close symbiotic relationship.

HISTORICAL CONTEXT

In the ancient world, contemplation was deemed to have a higher value than action. During Plato's time, the elites were thinkers and philosophers. In the story of Martha and Mary (Luke 10:42), Jesus was seen to exalt Mary as the reflective one, who had "chosen the better part" (Palmer, 1990:6). Then came the Age of Exploration and the Enlightenment, with the rise of Science, the Industrial Revolution, and urbanisation. More value was given to the active life, as people begin to realise their potential to gain knowledge (which is power), invent, change the world, conquer, and rule (Palmer, 1990:6).

In the spiritual renaissance of the last 30 years, from Thomas Merton onwards, we see the pendulum swinging back to the search for contemplative values. In the Protestant tradition, writers like James Houston, Richard Foster, and Dallas Willard call for a deeper and more authentic spirituality. Three decades ago, Richard Foster has lamented that "superficiality is the curse of our age. The doctrine of instant gratification is a primary spiritual problem. The desperate need is not for a greater number of intelligent people, or gifted people but for deep people" (Foster, 1978:1). He continues this call for a genuine spiritual formation that is authentic and pervasive through a transformation of the inner life, as opposed to the "all too familiar recipe of consumer-Christianity-without-discipleship" (Foster, 2003:1).

THE ACTIVE LIFE: CURRENT CONTEXT

In today's globalised world, those living in cities, especially, are constantly bombarded by speed, noise, and stuff, all of which can impede spiritual growth and disrupt the journey inward.

Speed

In today's urban world, work can no longer be restricted to the usual 'nine-to-five' anymore. With the rapid onset of information and communication technologies and social media giving instant access to the web, fast online conversations, breaking news, etc., it is difficult to retain boundaries around our working life (Barton, 2006:34).

A Christian Development NGO leader recently lamented that this is a major issue of stress and concern among NGO workers, having to cope with the overwhelming speed and load of information and communication.[1] Yaconelli described our busy schedules and fast-paced lives as silent killers. To him, this speed keeps us from spiritual growth, not sin, and the problem with the modern church is the rushing of growth (Yaconelli, 2001:110–112). Thomas Merton has said:

> To allow oneself to be carried away by a multitude of conflicting concerns, to surrender to too many demands... is to succumb to violence. The frenzy of the activist neutralizes his (or her) work. It destroys the fruitfulness of his (or her) work, because it kills the root of inner wisdom which makes work fruitful.[2]

As a 'frenzied activist' myself, this is a strong and timely reminder. I am learning how critical it is to consciously slow myself down, so that I might be able to hear those quiet whispers that are the voice of God (1 Kings 19:12)

---

[1] Deborah Storie, director of a relief and development agency, in a private conversation with the author on March 29, 2015.

[2] Mentioned in Palmer, Parker J. 2014. "The Modern Violence of Over-work." On Being. Retrieved June 16, 2015 (https://onbeing.org/blog/the-modern-violence-of-over-work).

Noise and Stuff

Most of us live in a culture that is permeated with noise. In my rapidly expanding home city of Kuala Lumpur, rapid urbanisation has resulted in dramatically increased traffic noise and the constant invasive sound of recorded music in malls and restaurants. Even the birds are affected! Research indicates that the urban invasion of noise is causing them to sing more quickly and in higher pitches and monotones.[3]

The modern church has also contributed to this noise, using state-of-the-art sound systems that are not only loud in volume, but also with dazzling disco lights and smoke machines. Ruth Barton likens our noisy religious activities to "an organised group of people crashing through the woods together, making so much noise that there's not a soul in sight!" (2006:33). This problem has not caused a spiritual dilemma; it has amplified it (Ibid)!

The demands of the prevalent market ideology have made us into a multitasking society, constantly wanting to achieve, perform, and possess more. This insatiable desire and the ensuing rat race generate a sense of restlessness and anxiety. Cities have become cacophonies of relentless consumerism: 24-hour eateries, kiosks, shopping centres, factories, and clinics. Hence our need to create spaces where quiet contemplation—so vital to the physical and spiritual health—is possible.

THE INWARD JOURNEY:
THE CALL TO CONTEMPLATION, SILENCE AND SOLITUDE

The call to contemplation is a call to a state or condition, where there is stillness, silence, and solitude; where there is a "renovation" of the heart, where we find our true selves; where the divine and the human meet; where the world of time touches the world of eternity; where our soul can be embraced like the prodigal son/daughter, falling into the loving arms of the Father.

---

[3] This is from a talk given by Winkett, Lucy. 2010. "The Sound of Our Wounds." Greenbelt. Retrieved May 15, 2015 (http://www.greenbelt.org.uk/media/talks/15694-lucy-winkett).

Contemplation is prayer as being. In contemplation, we rest in the presence of the One whose word and presence has invited us to a transforming embrace. It is "a gift of being in and with God that allows subsequent and very important doing to flow from this quite still centre, a movement form conversation to communion" (Benner, 2010:54).

The Terrain of the Heart

The heart, being the focus of transformation, is the secret place within us where our spirit, soul, and body come together in a unity of the self, even as we are called to love God with our whole heart, mind, soul, and strength (Luke 10:27; Nouwen, 2011a:xvii). In the Scriptures, the heart is the symbol of one's whole being. It is the place

> ... where the human and the divine intersect—the place of deepest searching and the place where we discover our most authentic desires, find our ultimate identity and perceive accurately the deepest realities. It reveals how we spend our time (Luke 10:38–42), where we store our treasure (Matt. 6:19–21) and how we live out our relationships (Rom. 12:18). (Groody, 2009:262)

St. Theresa of Avila calls this intuitive faculty the door to the interior castle, while Meister Eckhart calls it the "spark of the soul", with which one recognises the transformation into divine life, "the birth of God within the inner person" (Painadath, 2014:21, 26).

Facing Our 'Demons'

We battle not only external sounds but also the internal noise in our heads. Richard Rohr says almost all humans have Obsessive Compulsive Disorder (OCD) of the mind.[4] Lane suggested that the desert monks' retreat was not so much from the external world, but rather from an inner world of "ego-centeredness needing constant approval, driven by compulsive behaviour,

---

[4] Rohr, Richard. 2015. "Solitude and Silence." Retrieved May 5, 2015 (https://cac.org/solitude-and-silence-2015-05-05).

frantic in its effort to attend to a self-image that always required mending"
(1998:166).

Foster's call to reject those delusions of grandeur that say we are the
only ones who can save the world may have particular relevance to those
of us committed to serving the people whom society so readily pushes into
social and economic wastelands, for we run the danger of being deceived
by the inane notion that action is the only reality (1981:78, 89, 91). We
are all too familiar with our discontented souls, unhappy with our looks,
our bank accounts, our grades, even our age. Young people are miserable
because they are not yet 21, and older people are miserable because they
have passed it, and "that leaves most of us in misery most of the time!"
(Ibid).

In silence, we are forced to confront our demons. The Apostle Paul
talks about the struggles of the soul and his wretchedness in Romans
7:15–24. For this reason, silence may well be the most difficult discipline
to practise and develop,[5] because silence is not native to us. It is a strange
and terrifying territory (Foster, 1981:89–90). Adverse circumstances and
desire may drive us there, but ultimately it is the Holy Spirit as Divine
Friend and "Divine Dis-comforter" (Beck, 2009:2) who leads us there,
even as he drove Jesus into the wilderness for 40 days (Mark, 1:12–13), to
love, heal, and liberate us from self-destruction (Beck, 2009:212).

Finding Our True Selves

Thomas Merton writes:

> What God seeks of us is His own image in ourselves. This image
> is not something we can produce by our own efforts... it is
> already there. It is the simple reality of our true being as sons of
> God by grace... we let the Divine image come out and manifest
> itself by the way we live. (Mulholland, 2013:13)

Often, it seems, the image we have of ourselves is determined by what

---

[5] Rogers, Dennis. 2009. "Spiritual Disciplines: Pathways to Christian Maturity." Retrieved
June 12, 2015 (http://bit.ly/1TCrTKp).

we do, what we possess, what others perceive us to be, or even how we imagine they perceive us. Alex Tang calls us to:

> ... distinguish and identify who we really are (real self or true self), who we think we should be (duty self), and who we think others think we should be (perceived self). We play games to distract us from the real work of reconciliation of our fragmented selves.[6]

Such games leave us with a deep emptiness and are ultimately pointless. We need God's help in order to discover who we really are. In contemplative prayer, Benner says, "God begins to take the undeveloped parts of self and weave them together into our true self that is being formed in Christ" (2010:56).

THE OUTWARD JOURNEY:
FOLLOWING JESUS AS PRESENCE

We are all too familiar with Christian activism, where we seek to follow Jesus in practice, in a whole range of activities like feeding the hungry or confronting social realities. There is another dimension of following Jesus as Presence that can be pursued simultaneously. We are not to take it lightly, as Augsburger describes this indwelling Light/Word as God's own immutable eternal Presence (2006:48).

So, cultivating Christian Presence means we bring this deeply-alive-God with us, to the communities we serve, to be fully present for or with the people in times of need, loss, or danger. It is like a hug for someone who lost a child, a smile to a prisoner. It is like holding a lit candle at a vigil protesting against another death in custody, worshipping, and interceding silently. Authentic presence is like a gift of one's self for someone else, like a hidden presence of love. It requires deep attention and listening. The following two stories will perhaps help us understand this more.

---

6 Tang, Alex. 2015. "Reconciling Our Fragmented Selves." Godspace. Retrieved June 12, 2015(http://godspace-msa.com/2015/03/05/reconciling-our-fragmented-selves-by-alex-tang).

A Reflection on the Stories of Two Women in Kabul, Afghanistan

In August 2001, a critical incident happened in Kabul. Eight foreign Christian Development NGO (CDNGO) workers were arrested because of alleged proselytising. They were hidden away for months before they were rescued.[7] It started with the arrest of two newly recruited workers, for showing Christian films to local families. This sparked a massive crackdown on all CDNGOs in the country. All projects were suspended, hence affecting all the beneficiaries; all foreign personnel were driven out, most CDNGO vehicles, equipment, and all personal possessions in residences were looted (including mine).

Some local staff were imprisoned and tortured while other workers were harassed. It is daunting to realise how a seemingly small action by two new overzealous workers could have such rippling and devastating effects on the work, lives, and livelihoods of some very innocent people.

While it can be argued that both the individuals and their CDNGO lacked wisdom and maturity, the question remains: Would true spirituality lead them to do mission differently? If they had waited and listened to the lament of the city, they may have heard the pain of women mourning the loss of husbands and sons. If they had listened to the senior workers and to the voices of wisdom from the past, they may have heard warnings and modified their behaviour without losing their passion for transformation. Perhaps an understanding of integral mission and 'conversionism' that is embedded in an appreciation of spiritual formation as a gradual, progressive process leading to transformation would have helped them discern better ways to share their faith and their lives (Greenman and Kalantzis, 2010:30). Moreover, a deeper understanding of language and culture is needed if the outsider is to learn how to read the pauses and hesitations in speech, and this is only possible when genuine care and empathy is married to many years of exposure.

---

[7] An unpublished Integrative Strand essay, submitted for OCMS certification for the MA in Missions and Development Practice, Oxford, 2004, retrieved at http://kvisit.com/Ow/nzE. Due to the sensitive nature of the contents, this file is protected and cannot be freely accessed.

Let us consider now the second story of another two foreign women in Kabul during pre-Taliban times. A bomb blasted their neighbour's house with eight people inside. They immediately rushed over to help. A young Afghan orthopaedic-therapist from the International Committee of the Red Cross (ICRC) was there with his team, searching desperately for survivors, but to his grief found none.

He did, however, notice the presence of these two women at the bloodied explosion scene, and curiously enquired about them. He was told that they were followers of Jesus Christ. This silent encounter sparked off his independent search for God, but it was only after his arrest (and horrible torture) many years later, that he related his story: "That was the first time I heard the name of Jesus Christ. I saw that they were really good people, and I thought I should find who Jesus Christ is."[8]

These ladies were there in the margins of conflict; they were present with the distraught families in their shock and grief. They would have never known the effect of their presence on that young man if he had not shared it after his arrest years later. Their silent witness reminds us of the real meaning of that approach to mission, which has come to be known as 'Christian Presence' (Taylor, 1972:227). As Taylor so aptly put it: "to live thus totally towards God for the sake of the world is a profoundly missionary and, indeed, redemptive way" (Ibid).

Their example also reminds us of the wonderful mystery and grace of ministry, whereby we go into the world to touch and heal people by our simple *presence* in the midst of their suffering, just as Jesus did with regard to the grieving mother of the young man of Nian when it was said that "His heart went out to her" (Luke 7:11–15; Nouwen, 2011b:136).

THE SYMBIOTIC RELATIONSHIP: TOWARDS AN INTEGRATED SPIRITUALITY

Action without contemplation is rootless, frantic, and exhausting, even if the goal is as noble and good as wanting to alleviate human suffering, and

---

8   Retrieved May 25, 2015 (https://www.worldmag.com/mobile/article.php?id=18822).

even when motivated by love for neighbour. Well-intentioned activism can result in the fragmentation of our souls, leaving us deeply depressed—devoid of energy, joy, and peace.

Was it precisely into such a condition that Jesus spoke with such compassion: "Are you tired? Worn out? Burned out on religion?[9] Come to me. Get away with me and you'll recover your life. I'll show you how to take a real rest. Walk with me and work with me—watch how I do it. Learn the unforced rhythms of grace. I won't lay anything heavy or ill-fitting on you. Keep company with me and you'll learn to live freely and lightly"? (Matt. 11:28–30, MSG) This wonderfully symbiotic relationship that Jesus offers enables us to sustain our love for God, neighbour, and self.

Augsburger's concept of a tri-polar spirituality is helpful (2006:13):

> The spirituality of personal transformation (the inner journey), the experience of divine encounter (the God-ward journey) and the relation of integrity and solidarity with the neighbour (the co-human journey with friend and enemy, with neighbour and persecutor) cannot be divided. Tri-polar spirituality sees all three (the inward, God-ward and outward) journeys as interdependent... inseparable and indivisible, each part defines and determines the authenticity of the other parts.

Other writers have used various metaphors and stories to describe this integrated spirituality.

1. Walking on two feet of love—loving God and neighbour (Rakoczy, 2006:4).

2. Christian spirituality and "mission" are the inseparable symbiosis of "breathing in" (spiritual formation) and "breathing out" (mission) (Mulholland, 2013:16).

3. The image of a kingdom flowing/reigning through us, spiralling into deeper reclaiming, revitalising, renewing... on behalf of others, sometimes in spite of others, always with others (Dawn, 2006:115).

---

[9] Or justice activism?

4. Two sides of the same coin: The integration of Caussade's "sacrament of the present moment" and Brother Lawrence's "sacredness of the present task"—a beautiful description of integral "Being and Doing" (Ibid:116).

5. The two realities: Intimacy with God and the solidarity with all people (in the disciplines of care, compassion and accountability) are two aspects of the indwelling presence of God and cannot be separated. "They come together in the physical space called the human body and are realised in community—the Body of Christ, celebrated in the Eucharist" (Nouwen, 2011a:98–99).

Taylor argues that as we alternate between intercession and worship, between communion with people and with God, "the image of the symbol merges into the image of Christ, without any break in stillness. This is the gift of the Spirit, the beloved Go-Between, the opener of eyes and giver of life" (1972:243). This gift is beautifully demonstrated in the following story.

A Reflection on the Story of Michael

Michael has physical and mental disabilities that required him to stay in a twenty-four-hour care facility. He could walk but needed assistance with almost everything else, and his speech was impaired. His mother suffered from bouts of depression brought on by guilt for not being able to care for her son.

One day, his father asked him to come home to see if his presence could bring his mother out her prolonged despair. When he arrived home, Michael walked straight to sit with her mother in her bedroom. He stayed with her for a long time in silence. When his father came into the bedroom, Michael pointed to a large flower vase and repeated over and over again, "Ca... ca... oak," which later his father realised he was asking for coke.

When his father returned with the vase of coke, Michael took a small piece of bread, then tenderly took hold of his mother's hand, dipped the bread into the coke and gently lifted the bread to his mother's mouth as he began stumbling over the words of communion. His mother's eyes were filled with tears as she took the bread. Within a few hours, she came out of her depression (Yaconelli, 2001:128–129).

Who but the Holy Spirit could have prompted Michael to take that bread and coke? Taylor's "Go-Between Spirit" was so present with Michael and his mother as they communed together in that few hours of timeless silence (Taylor, 1972:126). This is the Spirit poured out, even when we do not know how to pray, the Spirit pleads for us with "groans too deep for words" (Rom. 8:26). Michael knew what his mother needed, and out of the depths of his heart, he performed this unusual act of discipleship in simple loving faith.

CONTEMPORARY EXAMPLES OF CONTEMPLATIVE ACTION

There are probably many Christian individuals, CDNGOs, societies, and orders out there living out an integrated spirituality among the poor and downtrodden. Many doing tiny, unsung acts of discipleship, living faithful rather than successful lives, some unsearchable even by Google!

One such person nearer home is Dr Tan Lai Yong, a medical missionary-turned-university don from Singapore, whose selfless work in China won him numerous awards, even from former premiers. He decided to leave because of their exaltation of him, which he considered to be dangerous for his soul.[10] He values community, rather than exclusivity; "we just need our daily bread and to learn the value of humility". At 53 years of age, he has no house to his name and no car; he owns only one pair of jeans and he hangs around with foreign workers, gravediggers, elderly people, disabled folks, and urban poor flat dwellers (Ibid). His action of downward mobility and voluntary poverty reminds us of the Franciscan way—of depth, breadth,

---

[10]   NUS News. Retrieved June 12, 2015 (http://news.nus.edu.sg/images/resources/news/2014/2014-04/2014-04-04/SAINT-st-4apr-pA25.pdf).

and process—"the process for staying at the centre: entering into the world of human powerlessness".[11]

Another example is the New Friars (or apostolic orders or neo-mendicants), an expression of a renewal movement,[12] predominantly found in Asia, Latin America, and Africa. Their aim is to plant such communities in the global margins by

> ... artistic, entrepreneurial, international, ecumenical, contemplative misfits... with a vision to see the flourishing of God's shalom among commercial sex workers, refugees, street kids and their neighbours trapped in poverty—communities committed to work towards systemic change in the halls of power... living out the signs of incarnation, mission, margin, devotion and community. (Bessenecker, 2010: 22)

These modern-day mendicants are committed to a radical pursuit of intimacy with Jesus through individual and collective rhythms of prayer, Sabbath, silence, and solitude, as well as radical, enthusiastic engagement with their neighbours and neighbourhoods (Ibid:107).

REFLECTIONS: THE CALL TO SELF

Silence in contemplation feels too much like wasting time—how can we sit and do nothing when people around us are neglected, exploited, or dying in custody? How can we abandon our indigenous brethren, displaced and suffering because of corruption in the high places?

Yet in stillness I am reminded to practise the kind of trust the prophets talked about in Isaiah 30:15, "In returning and rest you shall be saved; in

---

[11] Rohr, Richard. (2015). "Depth, Breadth, and Process." Retrieved June 19, 2015 (http://myemail.constantcontact.com/Richard-Rohr-s-Meditation--Depth--Breadth--and-Process.html?soid=1103098668616&aid=l08V8jFkVs8).

[12] Their members include InnerCHANGE, Servants To Asia's Urban Poor, WMF (Word Made Flesh), Servant Partners, UNOH (Urban Neighbours of Hope), which have taken the incarnational approach seeded (in presence) among dispossessed populations of young, urban slum dwellers.

quietness and in trust shall be your strength." Wasting time with God or waiting on God is not time wasted.

I am learning to see contemplative prayer not as a distraction but a necessity, a journey to a hidden wholeness. I am becoming increasingly aware of the violence of overwork, of the harm I can do to myself, and how not to "kill the root of inner wisdom which makes work fruitful".[13] In keeping silence and solitude, I am also resisting the noise (within and without) and stuff (consumerist tendencies). I am getting in touch with songs rooted in the groans of the earth. In slowing down, I can be fully present with people around me, learning to listen to the pain and joys of the urban poor families we walk with.

Most writers have often left out the "as yourself" when they speak about loving your neighbour (Mark 10:27). How can I love others when I myself do not know the Father's love? How can I know the silence of others when I have not learnt the silence of God (Taylor, 1972:229)? I cannot fight for peace with an unpeaceful spirit, nor struggle for a sustainable economy with unsustainable efforts (McLaren, 2011:237), because "the world changes as we are changed; peace comes to the world as peace flows in our innermost being and out through us to others" (Ibid:236).

REFLECTIONS: A CALL TO THE CHURCH

Evangelical activism poses a threat to spiritual formation when energetic service is emphasised at the expense of prayer, solitude and meditation (Greenman, 2010:31). The church is not immune from the prevailing culture of noise, speed, and stuff.

I echo Lucy Winkett's call for the Christian church to take up her historic role to call people to silence—"to witness to a different reality, one that doesn't need the endless distraction and clamour to communicate it".[14] There is a sound of lament throughout Scripture, which is more than

---

13   Mentioned in Palmer, Parker J. 2014. "The Modern Violence of Over-work." On Being. Retrieved June 16, 2015 (https://onbeing.org/blog/the-modern-violence-of-over-work).
14   This is from a talk given by Winkett, Lucy. 2010. "The Sound of Our Wounds." Greenbelt. Retrieved May 15, 2015 (http://www.greenbelt.org.uk/media/talks/15694-lucy-winkett).

grief or reaction; it is more like a protest of pain, a weeping voice. There is the cry of the earth—the cry of the oppressed, the refugees, the migrants, the widows, and the suffering children.

The cry is associated with rising inequality, corruption, failing economy, disintegrating social fabric, and the brokenness of human beings. The church needs to hear this cry and call for lament and repentance. The church needs to regain her gift as an oasis of silence to a distracted and broken world,[15] so we can discern God again in the midst of all these, embrace the pain and act responsibly with truth and wisdom.

Psalm 46 reminds us that even in the terror of crumbling mountains, of nations in uproar, we are to be still and know that God is God and He is with us; the God of Jacob is our refuge! This assurance brings not only personal calm, but also instils hope for the tired, disillusioned, and fragmented communities in my beloved country.

As John Taylor commented of the church:

> We speak with tongues of men and of angels in a dozen different committees; our gift of prophecy and knowledge defeats the politicians at their own game; our faith removes mountains of discrimination; our goods feed the hungry millions, our bodies are burned up in evangelistic zeal. Yet we lack charity, the only quality which makes contagious Christians, from whom others may catch the love of God. And charity comes by adoration. (1972:237–238).

He calls the church to be more attentive to God, to engage in the mission of the Holy Spirit by "being" rather than "doing", and to rediscover the prayer of stillness, which "deepens our communion with the Father and reproduces in us the *abba*-relationship that Jesus knew" (Ibid:240). For it is in silence that we can encounter Jesus as vivid presence, an actual co-traveller in life,

> ...which will result in the following practices that mirror the radical values of this most unique of all people, most insightful

---

[15]   Ibid.

of all teachers, most subversive of all prophets, most compassionate of all human beings, most courageous of all activists, most inspiring of all models, most intriguing of all mysteries. (Augsburger, 2006:40)

Conclusion

Action and contemplation should not be divided, but rather, co-exist in a deep and mutually enriching symbiotic relationship. They are intended to be interdependent and inseparable, one providing impetus for the other. "Our intimacy with Christ should drive us out into the world to tell the salvation story and to work for a more just society; and such work in the world should drive us to our knees in prayer and help us into closer friendship with Jesus as informs and impacts the other" (Campolo and Darling, 2007:203–204). Reciprocal and dynamic, it is akin to rhythmic breathing.

The world needs "prophetic women and men who are so deeply rooted in the love of God that they are free to envision and create a new world of things where justice reigns... where the old order of things has passed away" (Nouwen, 2011a:83). So let us, by the grace of God, heed the call to "learn to grow simultaneously in the life of prayer (contemplation) and in commitment to social transformation (action), to walk on the two feet of love of God and love of neighbour" (Rakoczy, 2006:4).

REFERENCES

Augsburger, David. 2006. *Dissident Discipleship: A Spirituality of Self-Surrender, Love of God, and Love of Neighbor.* Grand Rapids, MI: Brazos Press.

Barton, Ruth H. 2006. *Sacred Rhythms: Arranging Our Lives for Spiritual Transformation.* Downers Grove, IL: InterVarsity Press.

Beck, T. David. 2009. "The Divine Dis-Comforter: The Holy Spirit's Role in Transformative Suffering." *Journal of Spiritual Formation & Soul Care* 2(2):199.

Benner, David G. 2010. *Opening to God.* Downers Grove, IL: InterVarsity Press.

Bessenecker, Scott, ed. 2010. *Living Mission: The Vision and Voices of New Friars.* Downers Grove, IL: InterVarsity Press.

Campolo, Anthony and Mary A. Darling. 2007. *The God of Intimacy and Action: Reconnecting Ancient Spiritual Practices, Evangelism, and Justice.* San Francisco, CA: Jossey-Bass.

Dawn, Marva J. 2006. *The Sense of the Call: A Sabbath Way of Life for Those Who Serve God, the Church, and the World.* Grand Rapids, MI: Eerdmans.

Foster, Richard. 1978. *Celebration of Discipline. The Path to Spiritual Growth.* New York: Harper & Row, Publishers.

Foster, Richard. 1981. *Freedom of Simplicity.* New York, NY: HarperCollins.

Foster, Richard. 2003. "Pastoral Letter from Richard Foster: What is Spiritual Formation." Renovare, May 2003.

Greenman, Jeffrey P. 2010. "Spiritual Formation in Theological Perspective". Pp. 23–35 in *Life in the Spirit: Spiritual Formation in Theological Perspective,* edited by Jeffrey P. Greenman and George Kalantzis. Downers Grove, IL: InterVarsity Press.

Groody, Daniel G. 2009. "Globalizing Justice: The Contribution of Christian Spirituality." Retrieved March 7, 2017 (http://www3.nd.edu/~dgroody/Published%20 Works/Journal%20Articles/files/Groody%20IRM%20Article.pdf).

Lane, Belden. 1998. *The Solace of Fierce Landscapes: Exploring Desert and Mountain Spirituality.* Oxford: Oxford University Press.

McLaren, Brian D. 2011. *Naked Spirituality: A Life With God in 12 Simple Words.* New York, NY: HarperCollins Publishers.

Mulholland, Robert M. 2013. "Spiritual Formation in Christ and Mission with Christ." *Journal of Spiritual Formation & Soul Care* 6(1):11–17.

Nouwen, Henri J. M. 2011a. *Spiritual Formation: Following the Movements of the Spirit.* London: SPCK.

Nouwen, Henri J. M. 2011b. *Spiritual Direction: Wisdom for the Long Walk of Faith.* London: SPCK.

Painadath, Sebastian. 2014. *Spiritual Co-pilgrims: Towards a Christian Spirituality in Dialogue With Asian Religions.* Manila, Clarinet Publications.

Palmer, Parker J. 1990. *The Active Life: A Spirituality of Work, Creativity, and Caring.* San Francisco, CA: Jossey-Bass.

Rakoczy, Susan. 2006. *Great Mystics and Social Justice: Walking on the Two Feet of Love.* Mahwa, NJ: Paulist Press.

Taylor, John V. 1972. *The Go-Between God: The Holy Spirit and Christian Mission.* London: SCM Press.

Yaconelli, Michael. 2001. *Messy Spirituality.* Hodder & Stoughton, UK.

Living and Leading in Spirit and Truth

Steve Gumaer

The language of the true self and the false self has been important to me for the past three years. This paper is born out of my own realization that my false self was and continues to hijack me, perennially leading me into actual or near burn out, and robbing me of a satisfying relationship with Christ and others. In this paper, I hope to shed some useful light on how institutions and organizations that are dedicated to transformational work can foster a deeper level of transformational faith in the ranks of their members, while at the same time attempting transformational development for the poor and needy we serve.

The True and the False Self

In a paper on *lectio divina* and the special sort of prayer it is, David Benner (2010) uses the term "true self" in order to explain what occurs in a more contemplative state of prayer: "God begins to take the underdeveloped parts of self and weave them together into our true self that is being formed in Christ." The phrase, "true self", made popular by Thomas Merton (1972) in *New Seeds of Contemplation*, is a way of describing the self of eternity, the one of a kind creation of God who is wired for uniqueness and powerful expression and is not defined by material or external and expressive means. Merton elaborates:

> Our reality, our true self, is hidden in what appears to us to be nothingness... We can rise above this unreality and recover our hidden reality... God Himself begins to live in me not only as my Creator but as my other and true self.

A healthy self, a true self, first identifies with God's love and the gift of self that God has granted. My self is not something I make or defend or have to prove. It is, before anything else, a gift from God.

In Athens, Paul described why idols and external manifestations of the divine fall short (Acts 17:16–34). He says in verse 28: "For in Him we live and move and have our being. As some of your own poets have said, 'We are his offspring.'" Jesus also frequently references the kingdom of God. In Luke 17:21 he says that it is in us, not outside somewhere. The truth that sets us free is eternal, and unfolds as our souls awaken to the movements of Christ in us. In contrast, the "false self" is, according to Basil Pennington (2000), "made up of what I have, what I do, and what others think of me". The 'false self' is a construction, a way of being and identifying that is born out of a compulsion to survive and thrive in emerging complexity as one ages.

Many people are totally identified with the false self of childhood. An extreme example is people who have failed to connect with a primary caregiver in infancy. For them, the false self is powerfully born out of a disorder known as Reactionary Attachment Disorder (RAD). Three years ago, while trying to steer clear of breaking down and feeling desperately lost, I was diagnosed with this condition.

Whether it is born out of an absence of healthy infant attachment, physical abuse, neglect, or other early development trauma, the result is the same: A self is programmed in the limbic system that is not true in the eternal sense, but is a response to pain, threat, or vulnerability. As the child becomes a teenager and then an adult, these survival traits become more and more the conscious definition of self. This self is a performer, a conformer, a fighter, a pacifier; this self does what needs to be done to get the attention or response their primal self expects in order to feel controlled, safe, and loved.

In my case, the false self began construction in me before I even had the powers of self-awareness and articulation. Trauma is not required to make the false self thrive. The false self is the primary occupation of what writers of the New Testament, including Jesus Himself, call "the world". The world, or cosmos, is referenced 35 times in John's gospel. The definition is simply the created order.

In the New Testament, you know a reference is to the created material order of the world or the system and ways of thinking that dominate the world by context. John 15:19 says: "If you belonged to *the world*, it would love you as its own. As it is, you do not belong to *the world*, but I have chosen you out of *the world*. That is why *the world* hates you" (emphasis mine). "The world" here is clearly a reference to the natural world we live in, and at the same time, it refers to the world system that is opposed to God and goodness. This usage of the word parallels Paul's words in Romans 12:2, "Do not conform to the pattern of *this world*" (emphasis mine).

As Foster (1981) says:

> Within all of us is a whole conglomerate of selves. There is the timid self, the courageous self, the business self, the parental self, the religious self, the literary self, the energetic self. And all of these selves are rugged individualists. No bargaining or compromise for them. Each one screams to protect his or her vested interests.

It is unreflective living, acting without thinking, and becoming without considering what becoming is about that leads a person into the trap of "the world". The false self conforms, unconsciously performs its role and ceases to become. (It may be right to say then that sin is an act done out of unconsciousness.)

In Benner's book, Spirituality and the Awakening Self (2012), a very clear statement on how the false self is born and grows is this:

> The culture of family and society and the rhythms of our lives lull us into a sleep of complacency within the small, safe places we have arranged for ourselves. Seekers settle for being finders, even when what is found is so much less than what their spirits call them toward. Being and becoming are both routinely sacrificed on the altar of doing. The gentle but persistent heartbeat of our deep longings to find our true place in God is gradually drowned out by a cacophony of superficial desires, and we are left with a small ego self rather than an awakening self that is ever becoming in the spirit.

And this awakening of the true self can either be nurtured or stunted by organised community. Benner (2012) continues:

> And while nothing has the power of religion to transform and expand consciousness, it can also freeze development in the early stages of the journey and keep people in small places. This is always at the expense of the human spirit, which must be anesthetized to become comfortable with absence of self-transcendence. But that too is the power of religion: it can be either a force for good, or for bad.

HOW TO NURTURE THE TRUE SELF

All of my experiences have been transformational. Even the negative events and learning conditions of faith communities I have participated in eventually contributed to positive outcomes. It is a beautiful thing to learn what not to do as much as to learn what to do. Jesus said to the Samaritan woman at the well: "God is spirit, and his worshipers must worship in the Spirit and in truth" (John 4:24). The call to worship in spirit and truth indicates that Jesus Christ only relates to the true self. This again indicates that one can be completely identified with the manifestations of Christianity in culture and tradition and even call themselves Christ followers, but actually have no relationship with the living Christ at all.

When one becomes conscious of one's eternal and created self and stops living out of the false self script, there are visible effects. It is seen in a person whose actions and words are in complete alignment, one who is indifferent to praise or scorn, a person whose response to success and failure lead to the same place of humble embrace with Christ. These indicate that the true self is flourishing. Such a person has no dissonance between who they are and what they feel a compulsion to be. But what if the false self is the only self one is conscious of? What sort of spiritual formation is required to raise awareness of this imposter, and what are the implications for organised community life? J. R. R. Tolkien can help establish the meaning of my abstraction.

A POWERFUL METAPHOR

J. R. R. Tolkien's *The Hobbit* is the story of every man. In it, Bilbo Baggins of Bag End lives a comfortable, predictable, and adventure-less life inside a grass-covered hill. He thought he had it all. His life was so well structured that his neighbours knew what he thought without even having to ask. His climate-controlled cave provided all he needed. He thought his world was perfectly ordered—but then Gandalf the Great strode up to his round wooden door at Underhill to join him for his five o'clock pipe.

Gandalf ruined everything. He invited himself and his band of elves to dinner the next night, making Baggins host to the unruly lot. As evening advanced to the darkest hour, the group settled down around their leader, who led them in a song of adventures, high seas, raiding dragon's lairs, and the smell of mountain air. Their lyrics awakened something big in the hobbit. Tolkien wrote:

> As they sang the hobbit felt the love of beautiful things made
> by hands and by cunning and by magic moving through him, a

fierce and jealous love, the desire of the hearts of dwarves. Then something tookish woke up inside him, and he wished to go and see the great mountains, and hear the pine trees and the waterfalls, and explore the caves, and wear a sword instead of a walking stick.

Like most of us, the hobbit lived in a self-made prison that he called life. He was comfortable, soft, and oblivious. He did not want change or association with dangerous characters and unpredictable explorers. Afraid to step out and live, he had made his bed to die, thinking that what he had was the happiness and harmony of a good life.

Gandalf led a reluctant hobbit to prove himself as a man and discover his true self. By degrees, Bilbo Baggins surprised himself with his strength, cunning, natural gifts, and will to stand against evil. By the end of *The Lord of the Rings*, he had saved the world from evil by killing Smaug the horrible dragon and become the stuff of legends as a follower of Gandalf the Great.

THE METAPHOR APPLIED

In his Word, Jesus serenades us (like Gandalf did with Bilbo Baggins) with the same invitation to follow Him out of our comfort zone to become all that we were created to be. Sometimes life is a battle, but he is right there fighting for us and leading us to discover the mountaintops—and our full potential. Only in leaving the imagined safety of the hobbit hole in our hearts can we truly be satisfied.

And absolute trust is required to follow Jesus. If the mission we embrace depends only on our developed talents and traits, then eventually we will not be able to control the variables and the threat to identity will crush us.

To survive, my instinct is to keep a tight grip on the familiar and comfortable things in life. I think that by avoiding tension or challenge, I can mitigate the potential for failure. But that deception leaves me unhappy, bored and without purpose. At other times, the metaphorical hill

I hide in is a mask I create to meet the expectations of peers, family, and culture. At times I have hidden behind the face of what others define as leadership, instead of passionately pursuing the risky adventure that Jesus is wooing my heart to join. But trading my authentic self for conformity leaves me lonely and hollow. As the elves' song called to Bilbo Baggins' heart, Jesus is calling to the core of our beings to embark on the journey we were created to live.

I have read hundreds of books on leadership and management. Many of them resulted in slight changes to the way I organise, make decisions and lead my team. Covey's *The 7 Habits of Highly Effective People* (2013) inspired me to strategically arrange my time along the lines of my values. I changed many external disciplines in order to do the most important things first. One of his main points is that, "Our behavior is a function of our decisions, not our conditions". For a while, even my wife was impressed by the strides forward I was making as I disciplined myself towards change. I appeared to be growing on the outside and for a time was a more effective manager.

Inside, however, I was still the same performer. I constantly compared myself with others to feel better about myself, rarely admitted faults and when I did, they were sins that paled in light of my accomplishments. Admitting these minor sins just made me look more humble. Learning on any deep level was not possible because to admit that I did not have all the answers made me feel inadequate. I was not humble and Christlike as I thought; I was arrogant. My relationships were shallow and embracing the feelings of business and stress was much better than the irritating feeling that I was failing as a husband and father.

I did not have the self-awareness to understand what was going on. I was so lost in the script of my false self that there was no way to see how God uniquely designed me and for what reason I was born to this earth. I tried desperately to fit in the moulds (cosmos) of other Christians, missionaries and leaders, and felt defeated because I could never be as good as they appeared to be. But the Holy Spirit was calling to the deepest part of my heart to unearth my authentic self and abandon myself to his unpredictable call. I am, you could say, Bilbo Baggins of the Shire.

In John 8:31–36 (NKJV), Jesus talks about freedom. This freedom is not an external sort of civil liberty, but an internal freedom of spirit. He is not just talking about freedom from sin either, but a sort of freedom that breaks the mould of conventional wisdom to make way for a person whose tempo and direction are set by Jesus Himself.

> Then Jesus said to those Jews who believed him: "If you abide in my word you are my disciples indeed. And you shall know the truth and the truth shall set you free." They answered him: "We are Abraham's descendants, and have never been in bondage to anyone. How can you say 'You will be made free?'" Jesus answered them: "Most assuredly I say to you, whoever commits a sin is a slave to sin. And a slave does not abide in the house forever. Therefore if the son of man sets you free you shall be free indeed."

Like the religious leaders in Christ's day, I am often reluctant to change and grow. I am often stubborn. Change makes me feel insecure. That is because change is a threat to the false self; it is a threat to control. Honesty forces me to admit my weakness at the risk of rejection. Honesty does not feel safe, but the payoff is liberating. We can be confident in this: If we walk in the light, discover and abide in the truth as one of God's own branches, commit our entire identity to Christ and be real, we will discover the abundant life we all yearn for. I am not talking about salvation. I am talking about being real.

Matthew 18:1–4 (NIV) tells us how to do it:

> The disciples came to Jesus and asked: "Who is the greatest in the kingdom of Heaven?" He called a little child and had him stand among them. And he said: "I tell you the truth, unless you change and become like little children, you will never enter the kingdom of Heaven. Therefore whoever humbles himself like this child is the greatest in the kingdom of Heaven."

To some degree, we all hide in our hobbit holes of pride and fear no matter what our age. We plod along through our marriages, ministry, and careers, lacking spiritual depth while trying to appear successful by the world's standards. Then we wrap up our 80 or so years on earth wondering what it all was for. Some of the fruit of living out of your false self is divorce, gross sin, hypocrisy, embittered children, and regret. The cry of many people on their death beds is: "If only I had loved more, contemplated more, lived for the things that really mattered!"

The greatest risk is letting the adventure with Jesus you were designed for pass you by. It is the risk of ending your life with 'if only's. So pause on your journey now. What is the Holy Spirit saying to your heart? Is the Tookish side of your nature—your genuine self created in God's image—rising up in your stomach, screaming, "Let me out!"? Take the risk. Be real. Follow Jesus whatever it takes, so at the end of your life you can say with the apostle Paul: "I have fought the good fight, I have finished the race, I have kept the faith" (2 Tim. 4:7, NKJV).

And so, dear brothers and sisters, I plead with you to give your bodies to God because of all He has done for you. Let them be a living and holy sacrifice—the kind he will find acceptable. This is truly the way to worship him. Don't copy the behavior and customs of this world, but let God transform you into a new person by changing the way you think. Then you will learn to know God's will for you, which is good and pleasing and perfect. (Rom. 12:1–2)

It is ironic to me that the world we conform to, the world that kills our dreams and makes us fearful of risk gets our intense loyalty. We give ourselves to building a successful life as defined by society. And when we get it, then what? Solomon, arguably the wisest man who ever lived, wrote: "Then I observed that most people are motivated to success because they envy their neighbors. But this, too, is meaningless—like chasing the wind" (Eccl. 4:4, NLT).

It is time to follow the way of Jesus with abandon, declaring as he did: "Your approval means nothing to me" (John 5:21, NLT).

TRUE SELF PROCESS OF AWAKENING AND AWARENESS

Writing this paper has produced a sort of catharsis for me. It has made me reflect on what I have learned, the ground I have covered and the things I have discovered while fighting through the web of ambivalence to find a more satisfying relationship with God—one that is not dependent on behaviours and codified systems.

Learning to be a true person and learning to accept the self that is born in eternal love, instead of asserting a self that is based on perceived expectations and survival, is probably the single most powerful relationship step I have made. I am less defensive and anxious about what my leadership is, and my team is more confident that I have done my part to empower them and trust them. The ripple effects are dramatic, and can be seen even in my family.

The false self is not a state of being that can be killed or told to leave. It has grown out of unconscious needs. Whether the needs are acceptance, attachment, or self-affirmation, they result in the same production of one mask or another. And in some people's cases, they are so deeply ingrained in the self that identifying the false self is supremely difficult. It took a complete emotional and physical burnout, then intensive counselling with a psychologist, to begin to see the imposter I had become; the result of this false identification.

Now, when I recognise false self behaviours (like the need to control my environment and give at any cost to prevent a breach in relational harmony with people, especially loved ones), I take a deep breath and analyse this thought process in my head. Having considered the stem of the thought process, when it is the false self asserting itself, I envision shaking hands with it, thanking it for helping me survive and telling it that I no longer need its help.

ORGANISATIONAL SUPPORT OF TRUE SELF DEVELOPMENT

An individual is part of a community, and a community is a synergy of its parts. That synergy will be shaped by the code of the group, by the standards it uses to evaluate itself, by its leaders and their values. If the leaders establish a community based on false self behaviour, then the product will be self-reinforcing, both in the social environments and outcomes the community works for.

My question, still unfolding, is this: How do I as a leader lead a community towards spiritual awakening and true self behaviour? Are there things I can institutionalise that may contribute to the unfolding awareness of the true self? Are there human resource issues in place now that contribute to false self-reinforcement and behaviour?

Partners Relief and Development,[1] the organisation I lead, has 50 full-time staff and hundreds of part-time volunteers who come from all over the world. Our organisational platform is made up of six independently registered charities and one foundation. Our team community should be one that promotes the sort of positive growth that I have experienced, and yet I struggle to find ways to make that an institutional norm.

I have looked at our core values, our human resource management documents, and policy handbook. They are mostly what one would expect in such materials. They aim at fairness and coverage of basic issues, putting boundaries up to govern anticipated events and setting overall expectations. Comparatively, they are good, but not remarkable. In order to nurture true self behaviour, organisational documents are insufficient; it falls on the people who apply these documents to daily life to embody them in a way that properly inspires what synergistic outcomes we try to describe on paper.

SELF-DECEPTION, BEING IN THE BOX

Leadership and Self-deception (Arbinger Institute) provides insight into applying my thinking to organisational contexts. Instead of giving control and guidance techniques, the book places responsibility for most conflict and problems on the behaviour of the leaders themselves. Dysfunction occurs because people are self-deceived. Their lack of truthful self-

---

[1] See www.partners.ngo

awareness and displacement of personal responsibility is at the root of leadership distortion and entropy.

The metaphor the book uses to describe this state of self-deception is "the box". When one is in the box, they are in a state of self-deception; they are acting in an unconscious effort to protect their egos, their concerns and their sense of superiority, while the people they lead are demoralised by the lack of trust, the sense that they are not talented or capable, and the fear that this organisational culture cultivates. Self-deception and "the box" are summarised as follows:

> 'Self-betrayal' 1. An act contrary to what I feel I should do for another is called an act of 'self-betrayal'. 2. When I betray myself, I begin to see the world in a way that justifies my self-betrayal. 3. When I see the world in a self-justifying way, my view of reality becomes distorted. 4. So—when I betray myself, I enter 'the box'.

This is a secular way of describing the false self. Self-deception, self-betrayal and being in the box are all ways of describing the descent into false self-identification. At some point, reality is so distorted by this state of being that the true self is completely lost in a barely perceptible web of lies.

TWO SIMPLE OUTCOMES

Having carefully considered the scriptures and relevant books, I can only propose two major insights to help the leaders of organisations like mine excel at true self, or 'out of the box' culture.

1. Be the true self and exemplify true self behaviour with integrity in every situation.

2. Develop policies and procedures that give maximum freedom so that each team member has to decide on their own what excellence looks like.

Obviously, the starting point is to be true—to be the leadership, management, or team player that is the ideal presentation of humility and self-awareness. Doing this will naturally reproduce trust and respect, and set a culture that values humility over displaced responsibility. By giving broad scope to the applications of policies and their variations, we send the message that each team member's role is defined more by relationships and team needs than job descriptions and rules. In this way, a person *wills* towards excellence more than being pushed in that direction.

Jesus consistently pointed out to the leaders of Jewish culture and religion that the problems were not broken rules, but hypocrisy reinforced and justified by those rules, along with arrogance in the application of leadership. Jesus said in Matthew 23 that the leaders "strain the gnat and swallow the camel". They observe the minute regulations but disregard the spirit that those observances were born in. That spirit is humility.

In my personal life, I have endeavoured to be true. I pursue the truest expression of who God has made me to be. This to me is the flowering of spiritual formation. In community, my goal is to model the same organisationally. I have begun to implement policies that require willing participants who are motivated to develop the team rather than to simply fit in. Our member care manual is called "Self-care" because we want psychological and counselling resources to be embraced as each of us has needs, not because of a time requirement on a calendar. After four years of this, I feel we have made a good choice and anticipate more of this sort of thinking as we develop our structure in coming years.

> Living the material: Don't try to be perfect. Do try to be better. Don't use the vocabulary—'the box', and so on—with people who don't already know it. Do use the principles in your own life. Don't look for others' boxes. Do look for your own. Don't accuse others of being 'in the box'. Do try to stay out of the box yourself. Don't give up on yourself when you discover you've been in the box. Do keep trying. (Arbinger Institute, 2000)

REFERENCES

Arbinger Institute. 2000. *Leadership and Self-deception: Getting Out of the Box.* San Francisco, CA: Berrett Koehler Publishers.

Benner, David G. 2012. *Spirituality and the Awakening Self: The Sacred Journey of Transformation.* Ada, MI: Brazos Press.

Benner, David G. 2010. *Opening to God.* Downers Grove, IL: InterVarsity Press.

Covey, Stephen R. 2013. *The 7 Habits of Highly Effective People: Powerful Lessons in Personal Change.* New York, NY: Simon and Schuster.

Foster, Richard. 1981. *Freedom of Simplicity.* New York, NY: HarperCollins.

Merton, Thomas. 1971. *New Seeds Of Contemplation.* New York, NY: New Directions Publishing.

Pennington, Basil. 2000. *True Self/False Self.* New York, NY: Crossroad Publishing.

THE SCREWTAPE BLOG

Lyn Jackson

In His Abysmal Sublimity Under-Secretary Screwtape, C. S. Lewis created one of his most 'beloved' characters. Screwtape's letters to his nephew Wormwood uncovered some of Hell's best-kept secrets, enabling many benighted Patients to escape the clutches of His Father Below.

Recently, a strong resurgence of concern for issues of poverty and injustice has emerged in the evangelical church. For individual Christians engaged in justice and compassion ministries, keeping their spiritual vitality strong in the face of a world of pain and misery and a church that too often fails to embrace the vision of God's Kingdom has been a challenge.

This coming together of a concern for justice with a desire for inner spiritual growth is, naturally, an enormous threat to the Miserific Vision of Our Father Below, as Under-Secretary Screwtape would put it. So, reluctantly, Screwtape emerges from retirement to provide helpful advice to Practising Tempters.

1.

With some trepidation, I begin this blog in order to share with you, Shadies and Gentledevils, from the wealth of experience I have acquired in the service of Our Father Below. Trepidation, not because of any fear of technology—we've always been early adopters down here in the Kingdom of Noise, and what a great contributor to our cause the internet has been!— but because of the risks in committing to it material of a sensitive nature.

You will be aware of the disaster caused when a certain interfering fellow accessed some private correspondence of mine back in the middle of the last century and published them. My career very nearly self-combusted! However, I survived demotion and temporary banishment, and finally achieved the dishonourable retirement I so richly deserved. (For more about my stellar career, visit Infernal.com)

Our Technology Department assures me that this site is secure, and can only be accessed by registered users. (Forgotten your username and password? Click here for immediate annihilation.)

I emerge from retirement in response to a strongly worded request from Lower Command, from His Immanence the Director of Earthly Affairs himself. In spite of the tremendous progress we have made over the last century or so, a somewhat threatening situation has developed.

At present, the threat is not great; however, it is always best to nip these things in the bud, and His Immanence was kind enough to suggest that my wisdom and experience could be helpful to Practising Tempters in avoiding escalating difficulties. Naturally, I agreed. A large contingent of Infernal Police accompanying the bearer of the request helped me make up my mind.

The threat involves the confluence of two previously distinct, even opposing, strands of Christian thinking. As you know, the Church is one of the greatest threats to our Miserific Vision, but we have had much success in exploiting and even creating divisions and extremes, presenting as dichotomies ideas and actions that are actually complementary. This has been the case with what Mortals call 'spirituality' and 'social justice'.

In spite of the clear words of The Enemy in That Book of His, in spite of the life and teaching of Jesus himself, in spite of the example of so many ghastly saints and activists through history, we have managed to create an either/or thinking about these two dangerous traditions.

Divide and rule, my fiends. Separately, it is relatively easy to undermine a believer or a community by emphasising one at the expense of the other and getting our Patients' spiritual lives out of balance. Together though, they reinforce each other with the result that a truly spiritual activist is very difficult to defeat.

But defeat them we must. There are always possibilities, if we look hard enough. In this blog, I intend to particularly address the case of Christians who, through some diabolical slip-up, discover the vast stream of love and compassion (I'm sorry if you find these expressions offensive) which Our Enemy pours out towards those who are poor, unjustly-treated, oppressed and ignored, and become convinced of his intention that his people act to relieve suffering and work towards a more just and compassionate world.

Normally, such souls either burn out rapidly or, as they grow older, succumb to one of our best weapons, "contented worldliness" (Lewis, 1942). However, if fortified by spiritual disciplines and encouraged by continued spiritual growth, they can become extremely dangerous.

It is our job to see that this doesn't happen, and to that end I dedicate this small segment of cyberspace.

His Abysmal Sublimity Screwtape, retired.

2.

Let's start with the Patients themselves. For the sake of brevity, I'll call them 'justice Christians'. They are a persistent, irritating group who refuse to accept "a socially disengaged spirituality or Christianity" (Gushee, 2010:213) and insist on putting the words of Their Founder into action. Some particular nuisances spring to mind: Francis of Assisi, or Basil of Caesarea (Andrews, 2008:10, 27). More recently, Wilberforce and his Clapham cronies, that interfering baggage Gladys Aylward, Henri Dunant who took so much of the fun out of war, and Dorothy Day, who merely wanted to change the world (Andrews, 2008:63, 68; Gathro, 2001; Kiefer, n.d.). Such presumption!

These folk are by nature, active. They like to get things done. So herein lies the first and most obvious temptation: Focus their attention on *doing*, keep them busy and ensure that they feel that time spent quietly—in prayerful devotion—is precious time wasted (Greenman and Kalantzis, 2010:31–32). Before long, you can convince them that spirituality is for "super saints" (Campolo and Darling, 2007:60), not practical people like them. The busier they get, the less time they have to spend with The Enemy. They won't notice that the whole purpose for all their activity, serving him, is dissolving.

All kinds of delightful outcomes will emerge. A wedge will be driven between action and spirituality—always a good thing. We will have taught them, egotistical beasts that they are, that spirituality is somehow inferior to feeding the poor and healing the sick. The less they think of spiritual things, the less attention they pay their souls and the less inclined they'll be to arrest the rot (Peterson, 2000:330). And ironically, the less use they'll be!

The further they drift from The Enemy, the source of love, the better. That way, a passion for justice can be reduced to a loveless crusade, and anger, self-righteousness, and intolerance will soon appear (Campolo and Darling, 2007:182). Pride is such a deep failing for these creatures. In no time at all, they will have developed "delusions of grandeur that say [they] are the only ones who can save the world" (Foster, 1981:91).

Of course, they can't. Disappointment and discouragement will soon follow; they'll become tired and disillusioned. Disconnected from the sustaining power of The Enemy, they'll be less effective and their ability to endure and to survive setbacks will diminish (Campolo and Darling, 2007:182). Then we'll have them—bitter, angry, cynical, worn out, and frustrated. Delicious!

When the Christian life and mission is reduced to 'doing' without the necessity for or interest in a transformation of being, the Christian spirituality has been subverted and Christian mission becomes 'evil doing' (Mulholland, 2013:16).

I couldn't have put it better myself.

H.A.S. Screwtape, retired.

3.

My last musings gave a very basic but effective strategy for separating action from spirituality. This is fine as far as it goes, but some of you may have the misfortune to be dealing with Patients of a more theological bent. I'm quite fond of theology—lots of opportunity for befuddlement there.

One of our most successful confusions has been the grace/works debate. It's the same old principle—make things into opposites when they're actually complementary. Human beings have enormous trouble comprehending grace. They cannot bear to think that there is absolutely nothing they can do to earn The Enemy's favour. We, of course, can see how foul the little vermin are, but strangely, as I've written before, "He still offers them relationship with himself. He really loves the hairless bipeds he has created" (Lewis, 1942).

Some of them *do* get it. So naturally, we push them to an extreme— always a useful strategy. We make them so terrified at the idea of slipping into what they call "works righteousness" that they become in effect "paralysed by grace" (Willard, 2014:2) afraid to *do* anything. Millions of sweet little Sunday School children have learned Ephesians 2:8–9, "By grace you have been saved..." but never read on to verse ten, "to do good works". So after fruitful centuries of "Grace *from* works" thinking, we've got them nicely convinced that it's all about "Grace, *not* works", successfully concealing that the whole point is "Grace *that* works" (Augsburger, 2006:47).

This has two very beneficial results. Firstly, it makes individual Patients wonder if, through social justice work, they are really trying to *earn* their salvation. Better still, it isolates those justice Christians and Christian justice organisations from mainstream evangelicalism. A little dogmatism here, a little judgementalism there, and before you know it, you've got a very productive division in the Church itself, lots of mutual suspicion, and some wonderful opportunities for intolerance and bigotry on both sides!

Another intriguing possibility presents itself. The Patients who would never fall for the 'earn your salvation' pitfall may be enticed into the 'earn your relationship with God' trap. Spiritual disciplines are indeed dangerous to our cause. However, robbing them of their joyousness and turning them into mere observances is a proven winner. Make them into rules, rather than habits of heart and mind (Wright, 2010:172); moral rule-keeping like this leads to a censorious legalism that is very helpful (Cole, 2007:246).

I know it's difficult to believe, but these humans can actually think that their devotional practices in some way obligate The Enemy, rather than provide a channel through which they can receive from him (Thomas, 1998:50). Of course, intimacy with God cannot be earned through "the mechanical performance of obligations" (Fiorello, 2011:184). Deep down they know that, but a little effort on our part can turn the unwary into a right little Pharisee.

H.A.S. Screwtape, retired.

4.

Today I'll deal with one of my favourite topics: self-righteousness. The Pharisee was the splendid epitome of our endeavours at subverting religious observance into self-glorification, but more modest successes can be achieved, even by junior Tempters. The key here is to feed the creatures' misconception that it's all about them, for the more there is of them, the less there is of him (Peterson, 2000:28), which is a very desirable state of affairs.

You might think this would be tricky, considering that justice Christians have an outward-looking perspective on their faith, but it's surprisingly easy. Use that outward orientation to build up the Patients' dependence on external approval. Previously, I touched on encouraging the use of spiritual practices to impress God; they can also be used to impress others. Any spiritual activity, whether worship, devotion, or active service, if done for show, is "spiritually deadly" (Stassen and Gushee, 2003:451). It leads to misusing spiritual gifts for self-aggrandisement, which undermines not only the individual, but also the church. What The Enemy wants is "giving lives". What we want is "notice me" lives (Thomas, 1988:55).

"Human beings get a choice between serving God with purity of heart or using God to serve the idol of prestige" (Stassen and Gushee, 2003:451). We need to ensure they make the right choice—for us.

Human motives are wonderfully slippery. What starts out as seeking God can easily slide into seeking self-congratulation or the approbation of others, with a little nudge. Spiritual development is a "messy process" (Averbeck, 2008:33). Some say it's "God's own initiative and God's vital action" (Greenman and Kalantzis, 2010:24). Others believe that they "must do the hard work in the present of becoming the people [they] are destined to be" (Wright, 2010:140).

As with so many of The Enemy's fatuous statements, they're probably both true, but we don't want the prey knowing that. Emphasise the first, and you get indolent Christians who won't lift a finger. Emphasise the second, and you get Christians sweating away relying on their own willpower. Both are most acceptable.

If justice Christians do begin to flex their spiritual muscles, though they may not be seeking the praise of others, a little self-praise can go a long way. The human fascination with appearance is nicely illustrated in the gymnasium. So many would-be Mr and Ms Universes spend more time admiring themselves in those big shiny mirrors than in actual physical effort. Keep them looking in the spiritual mirror, feeling that they're getting somewhere. Then watch them crash!

Spiritual growth can so easily sabotage itself, without the necessary foundation of humility (Thomas, 1998:48). Fortunately, learning to be truly humble is a massive challenge for humans who really, deep down, think they ought to be God (Thomas, 1998:52). Instead, they must learn to surrender everything and place themselves completely in his hands (Groody, 2007:245). This must be avoided at all costs. True humility leads to love and unity, respect for others and a generous, forgiving spirit (Thomas, 1998:63–65).

What a ghastly prospect! I need a hot compress and a little lie-down.

H.A.S. Screwtape, retired.

5.

If we're going to make any headway with Patients who are attempting to balance their spiritual lives with their involvement in justice and social action, we need to address the critical issue of discipleship, the process that The Enemy, during his earthly sojourn, set up to train his followers. Its goal is nothing less than "to fill the universe with lots of loathsome little replicas of himself" (Lewis, 1942).

It's surprisingly effective, if time-consuming. The initial group of disciples was an uninspiring lot, but look at the damage they caused! Of course, they had Help.

It works by the immersion method. The creatures are invited into the circle of disciples (Augsburger, 2006:41), where they spend extensive time with the Master and with each other, to listen and learn and, largely through proximity, begin to change.

Those far along in the Enemy's service actually seem to turn into a different species of human beings (Willard, 2014:9)! Christ becomes their reference point (Foster, 1981:82), they begin to "think Christianly" about things (Wright, 2010:151) and eventually "the personality and deeds of Christ flow out of them" (Willard, 2014:5).

Well, that's the idea. Fortunately, discipleship depends on discipline and persistence, and these creatures find it very hard to persevere (Lewis 1942). The current passion of the Church for Programs is helpful; they are convinced that an eight-week course of watching some Great Man on a DVD, followed by discussion, is going to shortcut the hard work. Discipleship programs are mostly about rules for living a so-called Christian life, not spiritual transformation (Campolo and Darling, 2007:64). With shiny packaged programs and toothy promotions, we've managed to turn most potential disciples into "consumers of religious goods and services" (Willard, 2012a).

Jesus is, of course, central to discipleship, so we need to marginalise him. You may have seen my seminal paper on "The Search for the Historical Jesus" (archived at www.greatlies.com; Lewis, 1942). Human beings are adept at re-creating Jesus in ways that suit themselves, but have only a passing resemblance to the One they claim to be following (Augsburger, 2006:24).

They'd rather study him than get to know him. Encourage this: Turn him into the subject of debate or study, and treat him as a case or a cause, not "a Master or brother to be loved and followed". We want them in love with themselves and their own schemes, not with him (Taylor, 1972:241–2). Once they experience Jesus as a "vivid presence, a co-traveller" (Augsburger, 2006:39), we are in great trouble.

One of the benefits of the "Historical Jesus" strategy is that it encourages Patients to try to imitate him, or rather, their impression of him. This "What would Jesus do?" approach is kindergarten stuff, and we need to keep them there. We don't want them to get to the level of intimacy that asks: "Jesus, what do you want me to do?" (Augsburger, 2006:28–31). Turning Christ into a kind of moral good turns Christianity into a set of moral recommendations or a pattern of rules, rather than an "orientation" that directs human beings into encounter and engagement with him (Hauerwas, 1994:181–182, 204).

The lack of attention that the Creeds give to Jesus' life and teaching was a masterstroke. Straight from Jesus' birth to his death with nothing in between but a comma (Stassen and Gushee, 2003:130)! Wish I'd thought of that.

H.A.S. Screwtape, retired.

6.

In the next few blog posts, I'll tackle some of the specific ways in which justice Christians might develop their relationship with Jesus and succumb to spiritual growth, and suggest what can be done about it. Some of these methods are obvious; you would have come across them in Tempters' Training College. Others require a more experienced hand. Make sure you extend your repertoire, so that you can match the strategy to the Patient for maximum impact. (I believe there's an eight-week course available from our Training Department.)

First, the problem of That Book. What a nuisance it is when Mortals become enthralled by it. Our Bibliocide Department, however, has done some fine work, sowing confusion, fiddling with translations, encouraging hysterical debate over minor issues while obscuring major ones... Visit www.biblebasher.com for the latest advances in this area.

We've been successful in pushing people into corners where extreme views about That Book fester nicely—literalists versus liberals, that sort of thing. We do have a basic problem with evangelical Christians, though. They are committed to The Book, and demand a biblical foundation for everything. Sadly, when it comes to justice and compassion issues, there *is* an overwhelming biblical foundation. So, The Enemy has a great advantage; he can use their affirmation of The Book as his Word to show them his heart for those living in poverty and oppression, and so fuel their enthusiasm and give confidence to their activism. But all is not lost. There are still proven ways to achieve derailment.

Encourage a 'spiritualised' reading of The Book. Emphasise the Matthew Beatitudes, not the Luke version. Phrases like "What Jesus really meant was *spiritual* blindness..." roll off the tongues of many deluded preachers, undermining the validity of the justice Christians' desire to help those who actually are blind, lame, naked, or in prison. Keep steering them towards favourite passages, and away from sections that are challenging or difficult. Most Christians like passages that focus on themselves and their own needs, rather than portions about their responsibilities towards loving and serving others (Campolo and Darling, 2007:120). Of course, justice Christians do the same thing; they are preoccupied with the Prophets and neglect the pestilent Paul and his insistence on holiness and relationship with Christ.

Here are some more advanced ideas:

Encourage your Patients to read The Book from an analytical perspective, as they would a textbook. This will appeal to their "information-oriented rationalism" (Greenman and Kalantzis, 2010:29) and reduce Bible *reading* to Bible *study*. They will grow to treat The Book as a set of propositions or beliefs, rather than a source of "the kind of intimacy that leads to real transformation in [their] lives and in the world" (Campolo and Darling, 2007:119). Use any excuses to keep them away from practices like *lectio divina*, in which they will actually learn to listen to The Enemy, developing communion and union with him (Benner, 2010:48).

Steer them away from understanding The Book as the huge narrative of God's engagement with Creation. That Book is all about God, of course, but let them think it's all about them. If we can get them to see *themselves* as the "basic text", they'll just "consult it from time to time, like a sort of reference work" (Peterson, 2000:329–330). Keep their thinking concrete, rather than abstract. Don't let them look at broad, overarching themes; rather, keep them hunting for "proof texts" for their particular enthusiasms, so they'll reject anything that can't be justified by chapter and verse (Beck, 2001:44–45).

Here's a final perversion you might enjoy. Use This Book, designed for their encouragement, to *dis*courage them. Hold up to them the examples of great people of faith, and whisper, "You'll never be like that!" in their ears. (Don't remind them of the disgusting way in which The Enemy forgave their many glorious transgressions!) Take critical teachings, like the Sermon on the Mount, and point out that these are "lovely sentiments but impossible for practical living" (Stassen and Gushee, 2003:133). Above all, don't let them begin to comprehend that "people can actually be like that", when The Enemy's love has "occupied them effectively as a result of their having learned how to receive it in the deepest part of their being" (Willard, 2014:3). This will only encourage their faltering steps towards spiritual maturity.

H.A.S. Screwtape, retired.

7.

A human creature at prayer is a terribly depressing sight. That this thing of earth and slime can presume to enter the pure world of us spirits is outrageous; that The Enemy should have made it possible is beyond reason. But then, much of what he does is beyond reason.

I can't emphasise enough how dangerous prayer is. It gives Christians "that direct communication with the Father that Jesus knew" (Taylor, 1972:234). Prayer is the means he has given them to survive (Houston, 1989:59); in some mysterious way it releases his power into people and situations. It is a spiritual grace that facilitates human transformation (Groody, 2007:250).

The only really effective way to deal with prayer is to keep the Patient from the serious intention of praying at all (Lewis, 1942). Time pressure, scientific rationalism, lack of concentration, weariness, theological doubts—all these can be productively used.

For the justice Christian, keeping them off their knees is particularly important. Prayer and justice are closely related. "Justice without prayer quickly degenerates into frenetic social action", which eventually gets nowhere. But equally dangerously, "while justice often motivates [them] to want to change the world, prayer also challenges [them] to change [themselves]" (Groody, 2007:250–251).

Christians praying for justice present several opportunities. Firstly, we've done such a good job of creating Hell on Earth that the enormity of the issues can be devastating to Christians who try to pray. In the face of so much evil and suffering, where do they start? How can they expect their puny prayers to make any difference? We've trained them to expect so little from God (Taylor, 1972:46) that their efforts appear to them weak and ineffective. The Enemy may see them differently, but that's not our concern.

For some, the reverse is true. So carried away are they by their presumptuous certainty that they know what needs to be done, that they approach prayer as "a political shopping list, a platform, a manifesto"

(Elliot, 1985:23). This is definitely to be encouraged. Once they're convinced that their agenda is God's agenda, we can make them impatient with those who stand in the way.

Eventually, prayer can become "ideological buttressing" to support their particular ideology—a waste of everyone's time (Elliot, 1985:27). The drive to achieve, self-importance, restless ambition—all these work against real prayer. "A competitive spirit makes true prayer impossible" (Houston, 1989:44–45). Laughable really, that these creatures would think they can tell the King what his kingdom should be like (Elliot, 1985:31)!

Prayer expresses human dependence on God, for only He can truly create new realities in the world (Winn, 2013:74). When Christians pray seeking God's will, not their own, their inward life is being shaped to imitate the concerns and priorities of Christ himself (Houston, 1989:42). "To human animals on their knees, The Enemy pours out self-knowledge in a quite shameless fashion" (Lewis, 1942). Areas of strength and weakness are exposed, and Christians are freed and empowered to live out a more holistic gospel (Campolo and Darling, 2007:93). The synergy that results between praying and living is deadly to our cause (Houston, 1989:64).

So, my fiends, keep turning their gaze away from him and towards themselves. Preoccupy them with self-loathing (Campolo and Darling, 2007:94) or their own enthusiasms, or make them think prayer is a kind of lever to move God to act (Winn, 2013:73). Once they discover that prayer is not something you do, but a style of living (Taylor, 1972:227), our situation is desperate.

H.A.S. Screwtape, retired.

8.

Just thinking about the Church makes me smile. What brilliance Our Father Below has shown, taking the very thing The Enemy designed to herald his kingdom and turning it into one of our greatest allies (Lewis, 1942)! Here I want to expound some effective ecclesiastical temptations that will cripple the spiritual development of these justice Christians.

Belonging to a community of faith is very important to these pitiful creatures. Christianity is not "an individual pursuit" (Averbeck, 2008:43) or "a private adventure for the soul" (Augsburger, 2006:42). It's the place where fledgling Christians learn to fly, where growing Christians are groomed for service, where mature Christians mobilise and motivate others. It's where Christians learn about unity and forgiveness, patience, humility, and endurance (Groody, 2007:260); it's where they become other-centered (Cole, 2007:219). In short, it is a place where love should rule—"Since love is the primary virtue, community is the primary context" (Wright, 2010:144). Ugh!

We need to separate our justice Christians from this potentially lethal environment. Our Ecclesial Division has very successfully diverted the attention of the Church to divisive, theologically 'grey' areas—creationism, female priests, abortion, homosexuality—thus ensuring it pays little attention to "weighty matters" (Matt. 23:23) like justice and mercy. Many justice Christians feel alienated from their local congregations; the issues that drive them are seldom mentioned. Churches spend lavishly on espresso machines and comfy chairs, but give relatively little to feed the hungry and release the oppressed.

Our justice Christians shuffle from foot to foot during 'worship' times, staring at the Great White Screen and trying to see the God they know in the soggy lyrics and repetitive riffs that pass for church music. They endure psycho-slush sermons on how God wants to bless their lives and relationships, but don't hear about the blessings he desires for the poor. A little quiet whispering from us, and they'll soon be disenchanted and, even better, begin to think of themselves as somehow superior and more illuminated—and self-righteousness again rears its gloriously ugly head.

Now, you have a choice. You can keep them there, becoming progressively more judgmental and cynical, or you can encourage them to leave. Be careful, though. Just because they've left the institutional church doesn't mean they aren't connected with other Christians, the Church as the body of Christ. A fellowship group, a prayer group, or a justice or advocacy group can function as Church for these folk, with detrimental results (for us). Remember that the true Church is a fellowship, not an institution (Cole, 2007:220).

However, the institutional church is the perfect place to develop expressions of righteousness for show, with debilitating spiritual effects (Stassen and Gushee, 2003:451). If we can shift the focus off Christ as the Head of the Church, we can turn it into "a socially-constructed character-building agency" (Saucy, 2011:92) and manipulate the kinds of character *we* want to develop. And then there's hypocrisy. "How many stagnant pools of Christian respectability belie their calm surface, when hidden hurts and terrors lurk in their murky depths?" (Macdonald, 2000:18). If you've been paying attention, you will have noticed how easy it is to invent dichotomies that don't really exist. Combativeness, hostility, dogmatism, and insularity are all wonderful weapons to disrupt fellowship (Beck, 2001:42–44), and justice Christians are as prone to them as any other sort.

If your justice Christian is now ensconced in a small group of like-minded fools, another delightful temptation is possible. Any small coterie, bound together by an interest they feel others dislike or ignore, tends to develop the defensive self-righteousness of a clique (Lewis, 1942). The resulting spiritual pride is very destructive to humility and service. On the other hand, they may go searching for a "suitable" church to attend. Even better, since there *is* no perfect church, this attitude turns the Patient into a critic, whereas The Enemy wants them to be a pupil (Lewis, 1942).

H.A.S. Screwtape, retired.

PS: If you leave them in their church, keep a careful eye on their activities. It doesn't happen often, but sometimes, with Help, they do actually change it. "The last thing we want is the Church becoming a positive hotbed of charity and humility!" (Lewis, 1942).

9.

My fiends, we are about to tackle one of the most difficult and dangerous topics we will face. Already I can feel a certain powerlessness falling upon me. Even spirits far deeper down in the Lowerarchy than you or I have struggled with this.

Today's blog concerns the Spirit, the Third Person of the Trinity, the Helper. In the interests of knowing our Enemy before considering how to defeat Him, let's remind ourselves of the role of this Person in relation to our Patients.

Firstly, the Spirit *is* life and *gives* life, hence the enormous threat posed to us, who thrive on the stink of death. The Spirit enables the earthborn vermin to confess that Jesus Christ is Lord...

$%&)$%)^_&(^(&^&^%^#$%^&^%^%#%$@$#%^%^&&(^&*^%##&(^*^

(Sorry—major computer malfunction; had to reboot.)

The Spirit gives entry into the new community of the Body of Christ; the Spirit enables believers to pray like the Son, and empowers them with what is needed for the next step of obedience (Cole, 2007:244–245).

Misunderstandings of the nature of the Spirit are helpful. These creatures made of matter find it very difficult to comprehend the spiritual realm, let alone God as Spirit, hence the necessity of the Incarnation, God in flesh. The best mileage to date has been sequestering the Spirit in the "charismatic" or "Pentecostal" arm of the church, developing their dependence on greatly exaggerated outpourings of emotion, while at the same time feeding fear and suspicion of such displays in mainstream, traditional churches.

"Charismatics" can be enticed into self-absorption, where God is treated as a mere accessory to their experience (Peterson, 2000:337), while traditional evangelicals are robbed of the joy and confidence they could have if more conscious of the presence of the Helper. The tendency towards self-absorption among the former reduces the possibility of a deep, theologically grounded commitment to justice and compassion; justice Christians among the latter struggle to keep motivation and resist the temptations previously discussed.

When it comes to the so-called "gifts of the Spirit", we are on stronger ground. Human beings love gifts, and think in terms of private benefit.

Spiritual gifts, of course, are meant to be used in the ministry of the Body (Averbeck, 2008:35). Take the individualistic line. Encourage them to see them as *their* gifts as given to *them* for personal psychic growth, as a kind of personal therapy. Better still, foster spiritual pride, so that the 'gifted' Patient is seen as a sort of Christian celebrity (Cole, 2007:222). The higher they fly, the harder they fall, and hopefully, the more they'll bring down with them!

Those far along in the Enemy's service have learned to allow the Spirit to invade every aspect of their lives, and exhibit the energy and passion that makes them so destructive (Campolo and Darling, 2007:7). They know that they themselves cannot actually *do* spiritual formation, only the Spirit can (Averbeck, 2008:34). It is our job to keep as few of our Patients from realising this as possible.

H.A.S. Screwtape, retired.

10.

I'd like to return to that phrase at the end of the last blog post—the image of the Spirit *invading* every aspect of the Patients' lives. This is the last thing we want. What really gladdens Our Father's heart is when human creatures divide their lives into tidy segments and ensure that their spiritual lives occupy a smaller and smaller proportion of the whole. The great thing is to prevent them from *doing* anything (Lewis, 1942), but this isn't likely with the justice Christian. With them, we need to prevent the doing from being an integral part of their character or pervert the motivation behind the doing.

Take charitable deeds, for example. The creatures are a sordid mixture of benevolence and malice. We need to direct the malevolence towards their immediate neighbours, and the benevolence outwards towards people they don't know. Then "the malice becomes wholly real, and the benevolence largely imaginary" (Lewis, 1942).

Above all, keep them from actually knowing any poor people, or being involved with the poor in their own neighbourhoods (Elliot, 1985:29).

Otherwise, true self-giving love might develop, and then we'd be in dire straits!

"Self-denial" is not a popular topic among Christians, even justice Christians, but it's absolutely essential for spiritual development (Willard, 2012b:64ff). It helps them distinguish between what they really need and what their consumerist society says they need (Groody, 2007:247), and reframes their priorities in a God-ward direction in a most despicable way. Well then, we must attack it. If the sheer weight of advertising and social expectations doesn't get them (and it might not, as they are so boringly focused on the needs of others), try confusing them with competing issues and complexities.

For example, they need a new pair of shoes. They could buy a cheap pair, made by teenage girls in a sweatshop in Asia; that would be frugal, and they could give away the money they save. But then they would be complicit in the exploitation of children. So, buy an expensive pair, and now the children are out of work and starving. See what I mean? All this is most entertaining. People who talk about simplicity of lifestyle don't realise the fun we can have with it.

But we're not here to enjoy ourselves. There is serious work to be done. Generally, there's very little difference between the actual lives of Christians and those of other people. There are few "visible markers of holiness" (Goldingay, 2009:620) and that's a good thing.

Beware that they don't develop some, like keeping the Sabbath, for example, or refusing to go shopping (Goldingay, 2009:648, 650). And if they do begin to really put others first, make sure that these acts of self-denial become "dreary and deadly", still more exercises in self-righteousness (Willard, 2012b:67).

Make sure they never learn the art of saying no (Peterson, 2000:335). Keep their lives full of clutter—with things, tasks, ambition, other people's expectations or anything that will distract them from *The Enemy* and leave them confused, bewildered and vulnerable.

H.A.S. Screwtape, retired.

11.

Many justice Christians love to be active in the public arena, making them particularly susceptible. Politics can be seductive; walking the corridors of power, even if only virtually by 'clicktivism', can give them a tremendous sense of self-importance, which is very detrimental to their spiritual growth. And they might actually accomplish something. We definitely don't want this, for "the establishment of anything like a really just society would be a major disaster" (Lewis, 1942).

Even the act of standing up for justice and against inequity and disadvantage continues the wretched tradition of the prophets (Averbeck, 2008:47) and makes the invisible heart of The Enemy visible to the world (Groody, 2007:241). "It is a bitter blow to us... that any [person] who had been hungry should be fed, or any that had long worn chains should have them struck off" (Lewis, 1942).

Our justice Christians' sense of justice can, however, be used against them. We need to get them to the point where they treat Christianity as a means to an end, even the end of social justice. They rightly see justice as something The Enemy demands; work on them until they value Christianity because it may produce social justice (Lewis, 1942). Meetings, rallies, T-shirts, online petitions, postcard campaigns, policy development, and public events will mean more to them than "prayers and sacraments and charity" (Lewis, 1942) and will quite crowd out their spiritual lives.

Young people are particularly vulnerable to the excitement of public campaigning. But young or old, a great way of attaching them to Earth rather than Heaven is to make them believe that Earth can be turned into Heaven at some future date by politics or some other ideology (Lewis, 1942).

Fortunately, The Enemy is not yet ready to redeem all things, so political gains may not endure (Saucy, 2011:106–107). Disappointment lies in wait for those who are depending on temporal change. Their task, according to The Enemy, is to announce and demonstrate his so-called kingdom, not do the job themselves. They will keep on trying to over-reach themselves, poor little poppets.

Just as well for us!

H.A.S. Screwtape, retired.

12.

Some concluding thoughts, my fiends, before I shut down this laptop and return to my charming little Lakeside villa. I think I can safely say that, having completed my commitment to provide 12 timely, thought-provoking and educative blog posts for your edification, His Immanence will be pleased to release me again to my well-earned retirement.

That pestilent Paul had it right when he wrote about the supremacy of love (1 Cor. 13). Love is the greatest perversion of our Enemy; he really loves those loathsome human vermin, and he wants them to love each other. This is not natural for them—it needs to be a well-thought-out habit of the heart (Wright, 2010:157), and we must do everything we can to stop it from developing.

Constantly refocus their attention on themselves. Really, behind all successful temptations is their "basic addiction to loving [themselves] to the exclusion of anyone else" (Houston, 1989:70). Our modern invention, the doctrine of "self-fulfilment" (Goldingay, 2009:591) reduces the claim others might have on them and allows them to wallow in the tepid waters of self-satisfaction. Even our justice Christians fall prey to this. Feed their love of success, their love of winning, their love of power, their love of crusading, their love of going against the crowd, *anything* but their love of God and of neighbour.

The only way they'll grow in love is when they become more and more attached to The Enemy, through engaging with That Book, through prayer, through fellowship with each other, with the Help of the Spirit. We must use every weapon in our armoury to prevent this, as attachment to The Enemy means that they can "embrace the persons met with in life with the same attaching love" (Augsburger, 2006:45).

Do whatever it takes to keep the Self firmly on the throne, for if the

Self is displaced by the enthronement of God (Thomas, 1998:49), we are lost.

I have every confidence in your ability to avoid this dreadful calamity. With my very best wishes,

H.A.S. Screwtape, definitely and finally retired.

REFERENCES

Andrews, D. 2008. *People of Compassion*. Blackburn, Victoria: TEAR Australia.

Augsburger, D. 2006. *Dissident Discipleship: A Spirituality of Self-surrender, Love of God, and Love of Neighbor*. Grand Rapids, MI: Brazos Press.

Averbeck, R. E. 2008. "Spirit, Community, and Mission: A Biblical Theology for Spiritual Formation." *Journal of Spiritual Formation & Soul Care* 1(1):27–53.

Beck, R. 2001. 'Toxic Religion." *New Wineskin*s Nov./Dec. :42–45.

Benner, D. G. *Opening to God*. InterVarsity Press, Downers Grove, IL, 2010.

Campolo, T. and M. Darling. 2007. *The God of Intimacy and Action: Reconnecting Ancient Spiritual Practices, Evangelism, and Justice*. San Francisco, CA: Jossey-Bass.

Cole, G. A. 2007. *He Who Gives Life: The Doctrine of the Holy Spirit*. Wheaton, IL, Crossway Books.

Elliot, C. 1985. *Praying the Kingdom: Towards a Political Spirituality*. London, UK: Darton, Longman & Todd.

Fiorello, M. D. 2011 "Aspects of Intimacy With God in the Book of Job". *Journal of Spiritual Formation and Soul Care* 4(2):115–184.

Foster, R. 1981. *Freedom of Simplicity*. New York, NY: HarperCollins.

Gathro, R. 2001. "William Wilberforce and His Circle of Friends." C. S. Lewis Institute Report Summer.

Goldingay, J. 2009. *Old Testament Theology, vol. 3, Israel's Life*. Downers Grove, IL: InterVarsity Press.

Greenman, J. P. and G. Kalantzis, eds. 2010. *Life in the Spirit: Spiritual Formation in Theological Perspective*. Downers Grove, IL: InterVarsity Press.

Groody, D. 2007. *Globalization, Spirituality and Justice: Navigating the Path to Peace*. Maryknoll, NY: Orbis Books.

Gushee, D. 2010. "Spiritual Formation and the Sanctity of Life." Pp. 213–226 in *Life in the Spirit: Spiritual Formation in Theological Perspective*, edited by J. P. Greenman and G. Kalantzis. Downers Grove, IL: InterVarsity Press.

Hauerwas, S. 1994. *Character and the Christian Life: A Study in Theological Ethics*. Notre Dame, IN: University of Notre Dame Press.

Houston, J. 1989. *Prayer, the Transforming Friendship*. Oxford, UK: Lion.

Kiefer, James E. N.d. "Gladys Aylward, Missionary to China." *Biographical Sketches of Memorable Christians of the Past*. Retrieved 5 June 5, 2015 (http://justus.anglican.org/resources/bio/73.html).

Lewis, C. S. 1942. *The Screwtape Letters*. N.p. Kindle Version.

Macdonald, L. O. 2000. "A Spirituality for Justice: The Enemy of Apathy." *Feminist Theology* 8(23):13–21.

Mulholland, R. M. 2013. "Spiritual Formation in Christ and Mission With Christ." *Journal of Spiritual Formation & Soul Care* 6(1):11–17.

Peterson, E. 2000. "St. Mark: The Basic Text for Christian Spirituality". Pp. 327–338 in *Exploring Christian Spirituality: An Ecumenical Reader*, edited by K. J. Collins. Grand Rapids, MI: Baker Books.

Saucy, M. R. 2011. "Regnum Spiriti: The Role of the Spirit in the Social Ethics of the Kingdom." *Jets* 54(1):89–108.

Stassen, G. H. and D. P. Gushee. 2003. *Kingdom Ethics: Following Jesus in Contemporary Context*. Downers Grove, IL: IVP Academic.

Taylor, J. V. 1972. *The Go-between God: The Holy Spirit and Christian Mission*. London, UK: SCM Press.

Thomas, G. L. 1998. *The Glorious Pursuit: Embracing the Virtues of Christ*. Colorado Springs, CO: NavPress.

Willard, D. 2012. "Taking Theology and Spiritual Discipline into the Market Place." Retrieved February 6, 2015 (https://www.youtube.com/watch?v=uBh8Kz9uqG8).

Willard, D. 2012. *Renovation of the Heart: Putting on the Character of Christ*. Colorado Springs, CO: NavPress.

Willard, D. 2014. "Spiritual Formation: What It Is, and How It Is Done." Retrieved November 19, 2014 (http://www.dwillard.org/articles/individual/spiritual-formation-what-it-is-and-how-it-is-done)

Winn, C. T. C. 2013. "Groaning for the Kingdom of God: Spirituality, Social Justice and the Witness of the Blumhardts." *Journal of Spiritual Formation and Soul Care* 6(1):56–75.

Wright, N. T. 2010. *After You Believe: Why Christian Character Matters*. New York, NY: HarperCollins, 2010.

THE RIPPLE EFFECT

Rosemary Hack

The power of worldview to subjugate spiritual formation in regard
to gender-based violence

A s Bible-believing followers of Christ, we often fail to live up to
the biblical standards to which we ascribe. Even though we claim
to follow Christ and be filled with the Holy Spirit, our lives sometimes
degenerate into what is far from Christ-like behaviour or attitudes.

In the field of HIV and AIDS, one comes face to face with issues of
human sexuality, addiction, deeply-held prejudicial beliefs, and all the
accompanying mess. Friends battling the demons of various addictions
occasionally fall back into behaviour that they despise, but they have the
desire to change, and when they fail it is an aberration, not the norm.

This paper does not seek to address this behaviour. Rather, it examines
the habitual, ongoing abusive behaviour perpetrated by professing Christian
men against women. These men do not seem to think such behaviour
inconsistent with their lives as Christians, and often as Christian leaders.

Rachel is a beautiful, petite woman whom I met on an HIV training
course. She is married with three pre-teenaged children. However, despite

her outer and inner beauty, she is broken. She barely spoke, and when she did, you had to strain to hear what she whispered. About a week into our acquaintance, she was touched by something that was shared and an internal dam broke. She tearfully told us that the lead pastors (plural) of the church she worked at were serially raping her. She felt she had no right to refuse these 'men of God'. Andrew, a man from the church's leadership team, was also on the course.

Over the rest of the week, especially in the exercises around gender, it became evident that Andrew held deeply prejudicial gender attitudes. They were probably quite normal in the conservative culture in which he was raised. And it seemed that Rachel had been sexually abused since she was young; this was normal life for her as a female growing up in church.

Disturbing situations like this have far-reaching consequences. Addressing gender-based violence and inequalities are key to preventing further HIV infections and enabling people to access anti-retroviral treatment. Studies have shown that women who have experienced violence are more likely to contract HIV (Jewkes, Dunkle, Nduna, and Shai, 2010:41).

Although I live in South Africa and consequently a lot of my research is set around Africa, this is not only an African issue. Similar incidents around the world show that this cannot be written off as local culture, or an anomaly. In speaking with women around the world, I learn of many who are being sexually abused by their pastors, and in one case by a missionary father. There are also many families in the church in which husbands use the Bible to justify abusing their wives. And women often believe that they deserve this because they too believe that the Bible supports it.

These men are not 'nominal' Christians. They are professing, respected leaders of evangelical churches; they are men with whom we would fellowship and break bread, men we would learn from. They are not people who see discipleship as an optional extra (Willard, 2014:2). They are men who would teach from 1 Corinthians 6:19–20: "Do you not know that your bodies are temples of the Holy Spirit...? You are not your own; you were bought at a price. Therefore honour God with your bodies."

A 1992 study conducted by the Christian Reformed Church (CRC) in North America showed that 28 per cent of adults in their congregations had been emotionally, physically or sexually abused (Committee to Study Physical, Emotional and Sexual Abuse, 1992:321). In 2010, there was a 35 per cent rate of intimate partner violence in the general population of the USA (UN Women, 2011:8). This is 18 years after the CRC study and in the ensuing years, according to Human Rights Watch (HRW), rates of gender-based violence have soared in the USA (HRW, 2008), so it is not unreasonable to conclude that the rates in the CRC and in the general population are probably not substantially different.

What is wrong with our spiritual formation, that this can be so common, and that the levels of abuse in the church, which is meant to be a place of safety, are not substantially different from those outside it?

Something in our worldview is proving stronger than our spiritual transformation.

DEFINITIONS

This chapter uses the following definitions:

Worldview is how a person views and makes sense of the world. It is a person's often unspoken, sometimes unrealised, yet fundamental beliefs about reality. Consequently, worldview shapes and influences the way we think, and what we do. This includes beliefs about the origins and nature of the universe, the existence and nature of God, the purpose of humankind, what is good or bad, what is right or wrong, and a person's innermost convictions (Funk, 2001).

Both what a Christian is officially taught and what they observe contributes to their worldview. It is often hard to separate our Christian worldview from our cultural worldview; indeed it is often not possible, especially around such emotive issues as gender.

The worldview of many men leads them to feel threatened, and worry that women are taking over in all aspects of life, not least church leadership, which they see as their rightful domain. They worry about being displaced by militant, 'bra-burning' women who want to be like men.

Using fear-inducing language such as the 'feminisation of the church' and 'feminists' they dismiss a biblical theology of gender before they have even started to examine it. Women may also picture those who speak out about gender inequalities as women who ignore biblical teaching to submit to their husbands and male leadership, or fit into the role that they believe is appropriate and godly (Ayanga, 2012:85).

Spiritual formation and transformation are "the ministry through which we seek to stimulate and support the ongoing spiritually transforming work of the Holy Spirit in and through the personal lives, relationships and ministries of genuine believers, so that we all progressively become more conformed to the image of Christ, according to the will of God the Father" (Averbeck, 2008:53).

I also use the term *kingdom worldview*. By this, I mean a worldview in which, with renewed minds, we discern between what is cultural but unbiblical as opposed to cultural and neutral, and we are willing to take a radical stand against the unbiblical aspects of our culture. According to Romans 12:2, if our minds are transformed, we can test and know God's perfect will.

Gender refers to the shared expectations and norms within a society about male and female behaviour, characteristics and roles. It is a social and cultural construct learned through socialisation. The word 'sex' refers to the biological differences between men and women.

Gender-based violence (GBV) is an act of physical, sexual or emotional violence against another person on the basis of their gender. It also refers to violence perpetrated against men by women or by other men, and happens in all walks of life and religions, but for the purpose of this paper, I am limiting it to violence by Christian men against women.

Patriarchy, Male Privilege and The Old 'Normal'

Firstly, this paper examines some of the factors that contribute to and shape the worldview of a Christian. The Bible is set in a patriarchal context, so patriarchy is often seen as a biblical model for family life. However, the Bible never teaches this. Adrienne Rich defines patriarchy:

> Patriarchy is the power of the fathers: a familial-social, ideological, political system in which men—by force—direct pressure, or through ritual, tradition, law and language, custom, etiquette, education, and the division of labour—determine what part women shall or shall not play, and in which the female is everywhere subsumed under the male (Rich, cited in Okyere-Manu, 43:2013).

Men, raised in a patriarchal society, assume male privilege and power. They are often unaware of it—indeed, to be male is to be normal. This has been subtly and not-so-subtly underscored in many ways in the church; male-dominated leadership, restrictions on the ordination of women, the endless debates on the 'place' of a woman, women as the passive recipients of church teaching, the use of masculine language in the Bible and the pulpit. The Bible was translated by men, and the use of the male pronoun tends to portray 'male' as the norm and female as the exception, or the 'other', reinforcing common biblical misinterpretations around gender relations and gender value (for example the word 'human' is frequently translated 'man'). These misinterpretations are covered extensively in works such as Bilezikian's excellent book *Beyond Sex Roles* (Bilezikian, 1993).

However, a study of this nature would not be complete without a brief discussion of the Fall, the curse and the example of the patriarchs.

THE FALL

The influence of the Fall on the church's view of women cannot be underestimated. Tertullian, an early church father, said of woman:

> You are the Devil's gateway. You are the unsealer of that forbidden tree. You are the first deserter of the divine law. You are she who persuaded him whom the devil was not valiant

enough to attack. You destroyed so easily God's image, man. On account of your desert—that is death—even the son of God had to die. (Tertullian, cited in Museka, Phiri, and Madondo, 2013:115)

There are a number of problematic, far-reaching consequences of the attitudes behind Tertullian's statement. Not least, is it not amazing that a mere woman was more persuasive than the devil! And she (who by inference was *not* created in the image of God) destroyed God's image and was personally responsible for the death of God's Son. Part of the idea of a woman not being created in the image of God can be put down to the masculine language used in the translation of the Scriptures; for example, Adam being translated 'man', rather than 'human' (Stouffer, 2008:1).

In Genesis 3:14-19, God curses the snake and the ground. He did not curse the woman or the man, but the change in relationships, with God and with each other, was a direct result of the Fall. There is no record of man ruling over woman before the Fall, in the original perfect creation. Life, as it is after the Fall, is not life as God intended it to be.

The curse has now been lifted in Christ, the seed of the woman (1 Cor. 15:45). However, we still live under its impact. It seems that there are aspects of the curse that the church does not have any problem in mitigating—drugs to reduce pain in childbirth, the destruction of thorns and thistles in order to grow crops, etc. But the last line of Genesis 3:16, "and he will rule over you", seems to have been exempted from redemption. Indeed some would portray male domination as a blessing and biblical mandate. However, it is clear that according to this passage, it is a result of sin. These consequences of the Fall speak of natural consequences (pain, weeds and thistles, male headship), but not God-endorsed ones.

THE PATRIARCHS

The biblical patriarchs do not have a very good record when it comes to their treatment of women. Many were in polygamous relationships that led to much pain. It is interesting to note that God gave guidance to some of the patriarchs as to whom they should marry. But he never instructed them to take a second wife or a concubine.

King David's seduction of Bathsheba could more accurately be described as rape. However, history, literature, sermons and film depict her as a seductress, not as a powerless woman, who meets ultimate power in the person of the king who "'saw', 'sent for', 'took' and 'lay', all verbs signifying control and acquisition" (Classens, 2012:150). King David's record with his sons is no better. When Amnon raped Tamar, although he was furious, there is no record that he ever intervened on her behalf (2 Sam. 13:21).

Mary Stewart Van Leeuwen talks about her early days studying psychology. She noticed that there were entries in the textbook indexes for 'women' but none for 'men'. She says, "[O]ne thing now seems obvious about those textbooks: the standard for optimal human behaviour was simply assumed to be male. Women were different or 'other', and so needed special mention because they fell short of that standard.... They were as the title of a 1947 essay by Dorothy Sayers put it, "The Human-Not-Quite-Human". It is hard for a dominant group to critique themselves or their position. "As the old proverb puts it, a fish in water does not usually know that it is wet" (Stewart Van Leeuwen, 2002:23).

DEEPLY HELD WORLDVIEWS ON GENDER WHICH HAVE RELIGIOUS ENDORSEMENT

An Ethiopian proverb says that if you really love your wife, you have to beat her (Kiiru, 1999:5). In Swazi and many other Southern African languages, the word for wife is Umfazi, which means: "She takes her secrets to her grave". Violence against women is an accepted part of many cultures. Indeed, the idea that a wife should submit to her husband even if he is an abuser is alive and well in mainstream evangelical Christian teaching.

John Piper is a respected and influential pastor and author. When asked: "What should a wife's submission to her husband look like if he's an abuser?" he replied:

> If this man... is calling her to engage in abusive acts willingly – group sex, or something really weird... that clearly would be sin.... [S]he's not going to do what Jesus would disapprove, even though the husband is asking her to do it.
>
> She's going to say, however, something like, "Honey, I want so much to follow you as my leader. I think God calls me to do that, and I would love to do that. It would be sweet to me if I could enjoy your leadership.... But if you would ask me to do this, require this of me, then I can't—I can't go there."
>
> Now that's one kind of situation.... If it's not requiring her to sin, but simply hurting her, then I think she endures verbal abuse for a season, she endures perhaps being smacked one night, and then she seeks help from the church (Piper, 2009).

His simplistic response, if not so dangerous, would be laughable. The church is tacitly approving violence against women by minimising its seriousness, by their silence on the issue, and by their frequent blaming of the victim.

According to Chitando and Chirongoma: "Instead of being prophetic and insisting on justice, churches appear to be signatories to the 'covenant of violence' against women" (Maluleke and Nadar, cited in Chitando and Chirongoma, 2013:9). An American friend recently told me that her stepfather was abusive towards her mother. When her mother went to the church for help, the church leadership turned the problem back on her, telling her she was not being submissive. They then told her husband that she had come to them. She was 'forced' to attend church, but as soon as she had the chance she stopped attending. In Rachel's case, if her abuse were made public, she risked her husband leaving her and taking the children. In addition, she would have to bear the shame and blame for her abuse. The perpetrators, as religious leaders, held all the power of deniability.

Women in Zimbabwe report that the (male) elders within the church council who deal with abuse cases frequently take sides with the husband

(Ingwani, 2013:84). These are reasons for the under-reporting of acts of gender-based violence in the church. The church, which should be a safe place of compassion and justice, is not. Sometimes the fact that the church, which should bring justice, will break the trust of women who have been violated is more painful than the abuse itself.

> My deepest trust was betrayed, my self-esteem stolen from me—
> by that man and by the church that let him get away with it. The
> shame has been almost impossible to bear. I felt that my soul had
> been burnt out, leaving an empty shell (Macdonald, 2000:18).

A study of women lecturers in seminaries in Africa showed that seven out of ten women did not believe that the church was a safe place to get help if they were being abused. A further 17 out of 30 said that they think popular opinion agrees that the Bible supports violence against women (Hendriks, 2012:39).

A False Masculinity Formed Through Socialisation

Christianity and culture cannot exist independently of one another; this is not a bad thing, as the church needs to fit into a cultural context to be understood. However, at the same time, true Christianity is radically counter-cultural. Although we are in the world, we are not subjects of this world; He who is in us is greater than He who is in the world (1 John 4:4). We are subjects of another kingdom. It would seem, though, that in terms of masculinity, sexual violence, and gender relations, the gospel has become culture's prisoner and the other kingdom conveniently forgotten (Le Roux, 2012:53).

Stewart Van Leeuwen speaks of what psychologist William Pollock calls the 'Boy Code'. Although this is specific to boys raised in North America, it seems that many aspects of the 'Boy Code' are relevant to boys raised all across the world, although there may be local cultural variations. The 'Boy Code' speaks to male honour—and it shapes a boy's worldview of what it means to be a man. It subjects boys to a code of behaviour which, if they step out of, they would be seen as being less than male—in other words, female.

Firstly, no sissy stuff, hide your emotions, big boys do not cry or show it if they are hurt. If a boy acts like a sissy, he will be ostracised and mocked. Then, a boy must be a sturdy oak; he must be self-reliant and 'act like a man'. This is in direct contrast to a Christian lifestyle, which calls us to be part of an interdependent body and to be vulnerable to one another. Even in cultures where interdependence is a positive value, the male destiny is often to be the person that others are ultimately dependent on.

Closely related to this is the need to be successful, to be a big wheel, to have others envy you. This may be expressed on the sports field or in the world of academia—the key is to be at the top of whatever is the measure of success in the specific setting. Finally, to *give 'em hell*, to defend yourself when under attack, to take risks, live dangerously (Pollock, cited in Stewart Van Leeuwen, 2002: 97).

A British equivalent of this would be the 'lad culture' seen on university campuses, where 68 per cent of female university students in the UK report being sexually harassed (Phipps, 2014). Although this refers to university campuses, not churches, the sexist mentality behind it is pervasive; and these young men are the leaders of tomorrow.

It is not hard to see that these constructs of masculinity have been imported without question into our churches. Neither is it hard to see why men often regard themselves as without emotion, tough and needing to have status and power, sexual conquest and domination forming a part of that power. Consequently, women, who are 'other', are easy targets of male status and aggression. They are easy to wield power over, and it is widely recognised that sexual violence is about power, not lust. Maybe this is why Jesus' instructions on adultery and lust are so easily ignored.

Religion has a lot to answer for. Many religions, not least Christianity, cite scriptures to uphold the male status quo, power based masculinity and a man's absolute right to 'discipline women' and order them around at will (Chitando, 2012:75). It is hardly surprising that spiritual transformation does not have the radicalising impact that it should have when such a toxic mix of unbiblical teachings and male honour code forms a person's worldview. It is hard to displace a self-beneficial belief in a God-given superiority and mandate to rule, with the message of the cross, self-denial, and equality for the 'other'.

Although being socialised into a 'male norm' and seeing women as 'other' may be major roots of gender-based violence, there are other aspects of life and spirituality that also need to be taken into account.

DUALISTIC THINKING

If a patriarchal worldview affected things in the days of the Old Testament; then when the Greek, dualistic worldview of the New Testament was layered on top; it make things even more complex.

A 21st-century worldview generally communicates that we are primarily physical beings and it is legitimate to seek pleasure. However, there is also a popular move today to also see ourselves as 'spiritual beings', whatever our concept of 'spiritual' might be. These two ways of looking at life are very reflective of the context in which the early Church found itself. Our Christian worldview has been indelibly influenced by Greek thinking, both gnostic and hedonistic. Gnosticism views the created order as evil or inconsequential—what we do in the body does not have consequences in our spirit or in our relationship with God, and the goal is to escape from the physical and be restored as pure spirit. Hedonism sees the world as something that is there for our pleasure (Mulholland, 2013:12).

If we are not able to see ourselves as whole people and integrate the spiritual and the physical, then the temptation to divorce what we do in our body from what we are in our spirit, or to merely seek physical pleasure, is both powerful and deceptive. We may so divorce the effects of our actions from our spirit that we believe, much like the Russian monk, Rasputin, that we can wilfully sin with our body and then repent in our spirit.

Stassen and Gushee elaborate further on this dualism in *Kingdom Ethics*. Cracks appeared in the church's theology when Justin, in his efforts to curry favour with Emperor Antonius Pius, applied a dualistic interpretation of the Sermon on the Mount and Jesus' teaching to give to Caesar what is Caesar's, and to God what is God's (Matt. 22:21).

Justin tells Caesar: "[T]o God alone we render worship, but in other things we gladly serve you." Jesus as a Jew, however, had a different worldview—giving to God what belonged to God meant giving everything to God. However, Justin was a Gentile and as a previous disciple of Socrates and Plato, already had an ingrained dualistic worldview. It was normal for him to divide between 'spiritual' and 'worldly' (Stassen and Gushee, 2003:128).

The implications of dualism for our worldview are catastrophic. We have substituted a kingdom worldview with a Greek one. Political and economic structures, empire, colonialism, media, religion, etc., have exported this all over the world (often with the complicity of the church). This enables us to open the door for terrible selfish abuses. We can convince ourselves that upholding the power structures that reinforce male privilege, abusing those we see as less than ourselves, and wielding power over others are, if not fully legitimate, then not terribly serious and fairly inconsequential in the grand scheme of things.

CHARACTER MATTERS

It is clear that a kingdom worldview requires that we are whole persons—body, soul, and spirit fully integrated. To be holy in one area of life requires that we be holy in all aspects. Integrity of character begins with God in the Old Testament. Jon Goldingay points out that the word *tāmîm*, often translated as 'blameless', is more accurately rendered as 'uprightness'; a 'completeness' or 'wholeness'. According to Goldingay, integrity or wholeness is the first quality of someone who wants to spend time with God:

> It is thus an aspect of the commitment God expects of us and *assumes it is possible for us to offer....* YHWH expects our lives

to be *fundamentally orientated to what is right*, though without setting up unreasonable expectations about their being sinless and therefore blameless. (Goldingay, 2009: 600; emphasis mine)

From this we can ask ourselves, does God expect us to have integrity (wholeness) of character? Yes, He does. Does He expect us to be perfect? No, He knows us better than that. Does this then give us a licence to abuse, rape and oppress others? A resounding no has to be the answer to that; to behave in such a way is not *tāmîm*.

Following Jesus and being transformed into His likeness means not following our desires, instincts, and customs. We need to be retrained in holiness and righteousness. We are told that we should not be conformed to this world, but transformed by the renewing of our minds (Rom. 12:2). However, this does not happen without effort on our part. We are all so "squeezed into the shape dictated by the present age" that this takes effort, discipline, and spiritual transformation, as we learn firstly to think, and consequently to then act in a different way (Wright, 2010:151).

Being holy concerns more than morality (our actions). It concerns our heart, our thoughts, our motivations, and ultimately, our character.

CORRECTING OUR COURSE

I cannot overemphasise the need to change our thinking. Unless we recognise that there is a problem with our worldview in how we see gender, our spiritual transformation will be stunted. As N. T. Wright says: "It is one thing to insist on walking south when the compass is pointing north. But to 'fix' the compass so that it tells you that the wrong way is the right way is far worse. You can correct a mistake. But once you tell yourself it wasn't a mistake, there's no way back" (Wright, 2010:153).

Men and women, even those who are not abusers, need to see this as a priority. I was once on a small church-planting team in the Middle East, and the question of women serving communion came up. My (male) team leader's response was that he would rather not have women serve communion and 'play it safe' as he wasn't sure about it and "didn't have time to look into it because he was busy with other things". This is unacceptable: If a man is leading a team with women on it, he needs to prioritise looking into these things as they directly affect those on his team, not effectively rendering women as second-class team members. At the time, I did not think much about it, to be honest. I saw gender-based violence and discrimination as a problem of other religions, not my own.

Until we realise we have been trying to fix the compass, and it is important to rather fix ourselves, we cannot change. As we learn to think differently and to bring our lives into alignment with God's compass, our attitudes will change and we will and learn a new way to act. It is possible for our worldview to be subject to our spiritual transformation, rather than the other way around. This will not happen without effort on our part, but God has equipped us for holiness.

Eugene Peterson says that following Jesus and being transformed into his image means, "not following our own sin-damaged impulses, attitudes, whims, and dreams". Peterson goes on to say that we do not have to do what our glands or our culture tell us; we have the incredibly liberating freedom to say no. "The judicious, well-placed No frees us from... debilitating distractions and seductive sacrilege. The art of saying No sets us free to follow Jesus" (Peterson, 2000:335).

JESUS' RADICAL VIEW OF WOMEN

With Jesus as our model, we must radically change the way we view women and men. When Jesus was told his mother and brothers were looking for him, he told those around him that they were his mother and brothers, with one key addition—they were also his sisters (Mark 3:31–35). This is representative of the way Jesus saw and spoke of people; he was gender inclusive! In Mark's gospel, there are many positive examples of Jesus' interactions with women, showing women as having both understanding and faith (Gill, 1989:128).

The women and what they did	Lesson or reward	The disciples and others
◊ Peter's mother-in-law served Jesus.	◊ She demonstrated what discipleship was (Mark 10:45).	◊ Brought Jesus to her.
◊ Woman with an issue of blood.	◊ Demonstrated faith and was healed.	◊ The disciples ridiculed Jesus for asking who touched him (Mark 5:31).
◊ Syrophoenician woman.	◊ Understood Jesus came for Jews and Gentiles.	◊ Were ethnocentric.
◊ The poor widow who gave all her money.	◊ Jesus used her as a model in his teaching.	◊ They (and we) are taught by her example.
◊ Woman of Bethany who anointed Jesus for burial (Mark 14:3–9).	◊ Wherever the gospel is preached, what she did will be told of (immortality).	◊ They rebuked her harshly.
◊ The women who followed Jesus in Galilee, who came to stand with him at the crucifixion (Mark 15:40–41).	◊ Experienced the death of Jesus. ◊ Witnessed his burial. ◊ First to learn of the empty tomb and the resurrection (Mark 16:1–6). ◊ Commissioned as the first to preach the gospel (Mark 16:7).	◊ Betrayed Jesus. ◊ Denied Jesus, ran and hid.

Jesus displayed an outrageously open attitude to women, but the early church struggled to follow His example. They remember the names of the brothers of Jesus, but not His sisters (6:3), they recalled the name of the person in whose house Jesus was anointed, but forgot the name of the woman who did it. Mark seeks to redress the balance of contemporary Christian chauvinism and stresses the faithfulness of the women disciples in the ministry of Jesus. It would be impossible for Him to speak about people doing the will of God without making sure that it is understood that women were included (Gill, 1989: 129).

HOW JESUS HANDLED THE TEMPTATION TO POWER

Power and vulnerability are a dangerous combination. When they meet, it takes a person whose worldview has been formed by and subjected to God and His Holy Spirit to operate in true humility and resist the temptation to wield that power for their own advantage. The church cannot continue to allow its leaders and congregants to operate out of a worldview that ascribes them power, invincibility, and privilege.

> Christian spiritual formation must yield Christian disciples who are absolutely and stubbornly impervious to any temptation or enticement to sacrifice the sacredness of any group of neighbors for any private or public purpose, however compelling it may seem at the time. (Gushee, 2010:215)

Women have the right, in Christ, to be seen as human beings, worthy of equality and dignity. Their lives are sacred because they too are created in the image of God. Gushee quotes *Les Misérables*: "To love another person is to see the face of God". He goes on to say that "to hate, or degrade, or demean, or torture, or murder or ignore the suffering of another person is to spit in the face of God" (Gushee, 2010:226).

According to Augsberger, radical attachment to Jesus goes beyond knowing about Jesus or even believing in him. The secret is believing Jesus, believing what he believed, "of taking him as a radical example of rejecting dominance, violence or coercion; of investing your life in him by living out the reign of God on earth" (Augsburger, 1969:40). If we are to follow this model, our worldview will be subject to the Holy Spirit, not to worldly or inaccurate concepts of masculinity or femininity.

> I come to know myself truly as a spiritual being by knowing God. I come to know who I truly am by being known by God. I come to know others by seeing in them the reflected image of God, the Other. I come to know this Other when meeting God in others, sister, brother, neighbour, stranger, friend, or enemy (Augsburger, 1969:22).

Henri Nouwen, in his reflections on the temptations of Christ, takes a radical approach. His deep and rich book challenges our corrupted worldview and depicts true spiritual power as the willingness to put oneself 'under', not to wield 'power-over'. In looking at the first temptation, he talks about moving from relevance to prayer (Luke 4:4). He posits that leaders need to "dare to claim their irrelevance in the contemporary world" so they can enter into solidarity with a suffering world (Nouwen 1989:35). The second temptation, Nouwen sees as the "temptation to be spectacular", to be the person who has all the answers, to play the hero or heroine (Luke 4:8). The third temptation, in Luke 4:12, is the temptation of power and the need to move from "leading to being led", the willingness to be taken into painful places (Nouwen, 1989:51, 69, 81).

If our view of power were to be so radically altered, then abuse, perpetrated by followers of Christ, would be unthinkable.

CONCLUSION

A change in behaviour and deeply held cultural beliefs will not come overnight. Although I have largely addressed the attitudes of men here, change needs to take place in women too, as they are subject to the same influences, especially the teachings of the Church. Just because someone is female does not mean that she understands the dynamics that lead to gender based violence.

Transformation takes time. It took time for the disciples, even though they were with Jesus every day. However, as happened in the Transfiguration, there were moments of enlightenment, and we need those moments too. The Transfiguration was a part of the disciples' being healed of spiritual blindness, and undergoing a "radical transformation of vision and learning to see the world as God sees it" (Groody, 2007:243).

The spiritual formation of our worldview must redefine the way we do church. A survivor of gender-based violence expressed it this way:

> I long for the church to be a supportive community, celebrating
> life and God. Not a place to hide from, or conceal real suffering,

but a community that nurtures the courage to speak out against wrongs. If only the church could see human potential and life as something to grapple with and enjoy. And if only it could be a place where it's safe to be just who we are—real, flesh and blood and heart human beings, made by God, loved by God and redeemed in Christ (Macdonald, 2000:19).

An important part of the journey will be having leaders who are willing to openly address this issue from the pulpit, for the voices of those who have been abused to be heard, and taken seriously, and for a robust system of accountability for Church leadership (Stacey, 2015:22, 29). However, a cultural change has to start before that. It has to start with the way parents socialise their children, the way Sunday school teachers treat girls and boys and the messages they give. It is also vitally important that a theology and culture of gender equality permeate the teaching and practice of theological institutions.

Retrospective re-education also needs to take place, such as the use of proven programmes such as One Man Can, implemented by Sonke Gender Justice (Dworkin and Hatcher, 2013). It will take men and women, but especially men, who are willing to be unpopular with their peers, who are willing to be counter-cultural and choose a path of downward mobility. "Downward mobility puts its emphasis on people rather than possessions, on action on behalf of justice rather than accomplishments on behalf of the ego, and on the God of hope rather than the god of greed" (Groody, 2007:254).

REFERENCES

Augsburger, D. 1969. *Dissident Discipleship*. Grand Rapids, MI: Brazos Press.

Averbeck, R. E. 2008. "Spirit, Community, and Mission: A Biblical Theology for Spiritual Formation." *Journal of Spiritual Formation and Soul Care* 1(1):27–53.

Ayanga, H. 2012. "Inspired and Gendered. The Hermeneutical Challenge of Teaching Gender in Kenya." Pp. 85–92 in *Men in the Pulpit, Women in the Pew?: Addressing Gender Inequality in Africa*, edited by H. J. Hendricks, E. Mouton, L. Hansen, and E. Le Roux. Stellenbosch, South Africa: Sun Press.

Bilezikian, G. 1993. *Beyond Sex Roles*. 2nd ed. Grand Rapids, MI: Baker Books.

Chitando, E. 2012. "Religion and Masculinities in Africa, Their Impact on HIV Infection and Gender-based Violence In Men." Pp. 71–82 in *Men in the Pulpit, Women in the Pew?: Addressing Gender Inequality in Africa*, edited by H. J. Hendricks, E. Mouton, L. Hansen, and E. Le Roux. Stellenbosch, South Africa: Sun Press.

Chitando, E. and S. Chirongoma. 2013. *Justice Not Silence: Churches Facing Sexual and Gender-based Violence*. Stellenbosch, South Africa: Sun Press.

Classens, L. J. M. 2012. "Teaching Gender at Stellenbosch University." Pp. 147–158 in *Men in the Pulpit, Women in the Pew?: Addressing Gender Inequality in Africa*, edited by H. J. Hendricks, E. Mouton, L. Hansen, and E. Le Roux. Stellenbosch, Sun Press.

Committee to study Physical Emotional and Sexual Abuse. 1992. "Report 30." in *The Agenda for Synod of the Christian Reformed Church in North America*. Grand Rapids, MI: CRC Publications.

Dworkin, S. L. and A. M. Hatcher. 2013. "Impact of a Gender-Transformative HIV and Antiviolence Program on Gender Ideologies and Masculinities in Two Rural, South African Communities." *Men and Masculinities* 16(2):181–202. Retrieved May 10, 2015 (http://doi.org/http://dx.doi.org/10.1177/1097184X12469878).

Funk, K. 2001. "What is a Worldview?" Retrieved May 2, 2015 (http://web.engr.oregonstate.edu/~funkk/Personal/worldview.html).

Gill, A. 1989. *Life on the Road: The Gospel Basis for a Messianic Lifestyle*. Homebush West, Australia: Lancer Books.

Goldingay, J. 2009. *Old Testament Theology, vol. 3, Israel's Life*. Downers Grove, IL: InterVarsity Press.

Greenman, J. P. and G. Kalantzis, eds. 2010. *Life in the Spirit*. Downers Grove, IL: InterVarsity Press.

Groody, D. 2007. *Globalization, Spirituality, Justice*. Maryknoll, NY: Orbis Books.

Hendricks, H. J. 2012. "HIV and AIDS, Curricula and Gender Realities." Pp. 33–48 in *Men in the Pulpit, Women in the Pew?: Addressing Gender Inequality in Africa*, edited by H. J. Hendricks, E. Mouton, L. Hansen, and E. Le Roux Eds. Stellenbosch, South Africa: Sun Press.

Human Rights Watch. 2008. "US: Soaring Rates of Rape and Violence Against Women." Retrieved May 7, 2015 (http://www.hrw.org/news/2008/12/18/us-soaring-rates-rape-and-violence-against-women).

Ingwani, V. 2013. "An Exploration of Gender-based Violence Among the Shangaan People in Southern Zimbabwe: A Case Study of the Gazini Clan." Pp. 77–94 in *Justice Not Silence: Churches Facing Sexual and Gender-based Violence*, edited by E. Chitando and S. Chirongoma. Stellenbosch, South Africa: Sun Press.

Jewkes, R. K., K. Dunkle, M. Nduna, and N. Shai. 2010. "Intimate Partner Violence, Relationship Power Inequity, and Incidence of HIV Infection in Young Women in South Africa: A Cohort Study." *The Lancet,* 376(9734):41–48. Retrieved May 15, 2015 (http://doi.org/10.1016/S0140-6736(10)60548).

Kiiru, M. 1999. "You Cannot Catch Old Birds With Chaff: Women's Multiple Images in Proverbs." Wajibu, *A Journal of Social and Religious Concern: Traditional African Wisdom and Modern Life* 14(1).

Le Roux, E. 2012. "Why Sexual Violence?: The Social Reality of an Absent Church." Pp. 49–60 in *Men in the Pulpit, Women in the Pew?: Addressing Gender Inequality in Africa,* edited by H. J. Hendricks, E. Mouton, L. Hansen, and E. Le Roux. Stellenbosch, South Africa: Sun Press.

Macdonald, L. O. 2000. "A Spirituality for Justice: The Enemy of Apathy." *Feminist Theology* 8(23):13–21.

Mulholland, M. R. 2013. "Spiritual Formation in Christ and Mission With Christ." *Journal of Spiritual Formation and Soul Care* 6(1):11–17.

Museka, G., M. Phiri, and M. M. Madondo. 2013. "Patriarchy and Gender-based Violence: The Politics of Exclusion in Zimbabwe's Roman Catholic Church." Pp. 111–131 in *Justice Not Silence: Churches Facing Sexual and Gender-based Violence,* edited by E. Chitando and S. Chirongoma. Stellenbosch, South Africa: Sun Press.

Nouwen, H. J. M. 1989. *In the Name of Jesus: Reflections on Christian Leadership.* Chestnut Ridge, NY: Crossroad Publishing.

Okyere-Manu, B. 2013. "The Sexual Abuse of the Girl Child in Pietermaritzburg, South Africa: Rethinking the Christian Response." Pp. 35–46 in *Justice Not Silence, Churches Facing Sexual and Gender-based Violence,* edited by E. Chitando and S. Chirongoma. Stellenbosch, South Africa: Sun Press.

Peterson, E. H. 2000. "St. Mark: The Basic Text for Christian Spirituality." Pp. 327–338 in *Exploring Christian Spirituality: An Ecumenical Reader,* edited by K. J. Collins. Grand Rapids, MI: Baker Books.

Phipps, A. 2014. "Lad Culture Thrives in Our Neoliberal Universities." Higher Education Network. Retrieved May 16, 2015 (http://www.theguardian.com/higher-education-network/blog/2014/oct/15/lad-culture-thrives-in-our-neoliberal-universities).

Piper, J. 2009. "Does a Women Submit to Abuse?" Retrieved May 13, 2015 (https://www.youtube.com/watch?v=3OkUPc2NLrM).

Stacey, J. 2015. "Courage, Cost and Hope: The Report on the Past Cases Review (2013–2015)." The Methodist Church in Britain. Retrieved May 28, 2015 (http://www.methodist.org.uk/media/4409/past-cases-review-2013-2015-final.pdf).

Stassen, G. H. and D. P. Gushee. 2003. *Kingdom Ethics: Transforming Initiatives.* Downers Grove, IL: InterVarsity Press.

Stewart Van Leeuwen, M. 2002. *My Brother's Keeper, What the Social Sciences Do (and Don't) Tell Us About Masculinity.* Downers Grove, IL: InterVarsity Press.

Stouffer, A. H. 2008. *95 More for the Door: A Layperson's Biblical Guide to the Gender Reformation.* Winnipeg, Canada: Word Alive Press.

UN Women. 2011. "Violence Against Women Prevalence Data: Surveys by Country." Retrieved May 10, 2015 (http://www.endvawnow.org/uploads/browser/files/vaw_prevalence_matrix_15april_2011.pdf).

Willard, D. 2014. "Spiritual Formation: What It Is, and How It Is Done." Retrieved December 1, 2014 (http://www.dwillard.org/articles/individual/spiritual-formation-what-it-is-and-how-it-is-done).

Wright, N. T. 2010. *After You Believe: Why Christian Character Matters.* New York, NY: HarperCollins.

Lessons in Faith from the Karen People of Myanmar

Oddny Gumaer

*T*hey had just fled their village. Nothing was left. Their houses were burned to the ground.

Their belongings were either destroyed or stolen. (Some belongings would not burn and would have been hard to transport—cooking pots, for example. To ensure that they could never be used again, the Burma Army soldiers took their machetes and poked holes in the bottom of the pots. A family's most important belongings were now useless.) Their animals were slaughtered or killed in the fire. Their school was gone. So was the church.

They were hiding in the jungle. The only food they had was what they had been able to carry with them when they fled. It was raining and they were wet. Some of the children were sick and were coughing. The parents had to calm them with soup made from the water the rice had been boiled in. None knew how long they would have to run or how long they would have to be in hiding.

But it was Sunday, and even if all else was in disarray, some things never changed. Sunday was a day of worship. So the group of about 50 villagers gathered on the jungle floor and had a church service.

I was not there when this happened, but our friend was. He called us on a satellite phone and let us listen in.

For more than 20 years I have been working with the Karen people of Myanmar. Their suffering compelled me to get involved with their lives. Their oppression and poverty have been the main reason for our ongoing work in their villages, hide sites, and organised refugee camps. But it is their faith that has impressed me the most. In the Karen, I have seen a faith, commitment and courage I never knew.

I have watched them worship, heard their testimonies and seen their faithfulness to their churches for years, and I have wondered: Why does it matter so much to them? I have heard them explain their faith and I have been awed by how simple, yet how complex, it is. I have met them after everything they own have been destroyed and asked them how this affects their trust in God; they have just looked at me in utter confusion: "Why should we blame God?" they say.

I wanted to try to understand their spirituality a little better and find out what it is that fills their souls with such confidence and peace.

The Karen is the second largest ethnic nationality of Myanmar, after the majority, the Burmans. There is an estimated seven million Karen living predominantly in Western Burma, in the area referred to as Karen State, or *Kaw Thoo Lei* (A Land Without Evil), as the Karen themselves call it. Since the military coup in 1962, the army has increased the numbers of soldiers to 400,000–500,000. A policy called the "Four Cuts Campaign", which forced relocation and free-fire zones, were employed to take away life-sustaining resources from the Karen. When the Burma Army took over the area, the local people were forcibly removed to relocation sites, forced to labour for the military and used as human minesweepers. Women were raped; murder, massacres, and other atrocities were common. Thousands of villages were burned to the ground during decades of civil war. As many as one million people became Internal Displaced Persons (IDPs), refugees in their own country.

People express surprise and almost disbelief when I tell them that a high percentage of Karen are Christians. It is estimated that approximately 25 per cent of all Karen are followers of Christ (Neiman, Soh, and Sutan, 2015). One can understand why people find it strange that an ethnic group in a Buddhist country in Southeast Asia has a large population of Christian believers. Looking at the nation as a whole, only four per cent of the citizens follow the Christian faith. The number of Christians in the nations surrounding Myanmar is also very low.

Not all Karen are Christ followers, of course. Also, amongst the Karen, most would call themselves Buddhists. A significant number are also animist. Among the resistance leaders, however, there has always been a majority of Christians. Thus, much of the politics adopted by the resistance movement has been influenced by Christian values.

In *Eternity in their Hearts*, Don Richardson (1980) tells the fascinating story of how the Karen received their faith. For centuries, the Karen believed that long ago they had possessed a book, "The Golden Book", which contained the truth about life. The book was lost (or, some legends say, a white brother took it across the sea), but one day the book would be returned to them, and the truth about life would be found again.

In 1795, a British diplomat from the embassy in Rangoon visited a Karen village. The villagers immediately surrounded him with great excitement. He was the first white man they had seen, and they were sure he was the long-lost brother returning with "The Golden Book". They also believed that the Book would bring them in touch with their god, whose name was Y'wa. The diplomat, however, misunderstood the excitement and the Karen's request for a golden book. He told his guide and translator that they were wrong, and that he had no idea who their "white brother" might be. The Karen, understandably, were very disappointed.

Not until Ko Tha Byu, a Karen slave and former bandit, converted to Christianity and started sharing the gospel in the villages did they get to see "The Golden Book". Ko Tha Byu told the villagers that the white brother had indeed returned with the book. In the book was the answer to what they had been wondering for hundreds of years: how to restore their relationship with Y'wa. Within 25 years almost 12,000 Karen had become Christians, and they began missionary work themselves (Richardson, 1980).

Many scholars claim that the Karen's traditional teachings are a direct replica of Genesis. British missionary to the Karen in the 19th century, Donald Mackenzie Smeaton, argues: "Their belief in the character and attributes of God is absolutely identical to the teachings of Christianity, and requires no modifications save the teachings of Jesus Christ as the revelation of God and the Savior of man" (Smeaton, 1920:178).

The Karen did believe in one God, named Y'wa. He was the Creator of the universe. The Karen also believed that humanity had fallen away from Y'wa by eating forbidden fruit. An ancient Karen poem, one can read:

> Y'wa formed the world originally. He appointed food and drink.
> He appointed the "Fruit of Trial". He gave detailed orders.
> Mu—kaw—lee deceived two persons.
> He caused them to eat the fruit of the Tree of Trial. They obeyed
> not; they believed not Y'wa. When they ate the fruit of trial,
> They became subject to sickness, aging and death.
> (Richardson, 1980.)

In his book, *The Karen People of Burma*, former missionary Harry Ignatius Marshall explains that the Karen also believed the devil came in the form of a great serpent. They believed that God, Y'wa, was all-powerful and had created man and woman. He created heaven and earth, and the woman had been formed from the rib of man (Marshall 1922:215). Many more similarities have been found between ancient Karen folk belief and Christianity. It is no wonder the Karen was so ready to receive the Gospel! This was what they had waited for over many centuries.

Reading about their folklore and how God must have put eternity in their hearts gave me great confidence in his existence and love for the peoples of the world. All would have been well had they been left to live peacefully on their land, harvesting their crops, tending to their animals and worshipping God in simple bamboo churches. It would have been a perfect story with a happy ending. They found their lost brother, they got to read "The Golden Book" and their relationship to Y'wa was restored through his son, Jesus Christ.

But the history of the Karen for the past 50 years or more is the story of suffering, death and terrible betrayal. Not many people on the earth have suffered as much and for as long as the Karen. How has it affected their faith? How are they able to continue to worship a loving God when their lives have been torn apart in the most heinous ways? Why is their faith still so strong and vibrant?

SPIRITUAL FORMATION

"A good working definition of spiritual disciplines are those activities that we do that help us practice God's presence," says the *Introduction to Spiritual Discipline*. "Essential is the understanding that God is working in our lives. It is grace that has developed so the discipline can develop."

Spiritual formation is much more than a list of activities and disciplines one practises in order to obtain spiritual growth. The above definition is a helpful check on one's practices. Does this activity help me practise God's presence, and if it does, is it by his grace? Does it produce the 'fruit of the Spirit'?

Greenman emphasises that spiritual formation is shaping us into the likeness of Christ. He also says that rather than it being a search for spiritual health within ourselves, it is a response to God's grace in our lives (Greenman, 2010:23–35). Coming to this realisation, however, will require certain spiritual disciplines, such as prayer and confession, fasting, biblical meditation, and corporate participation in the congregation's shared life of worship, fellowship, and teaching (Greenman, 2010:24–26).

In observing the faith of the Karen Christians, I have seen that they have learned this, and they practice ancient spiritual disciplines with great dedication, frequency, and structure. Some may say that they have kept their faith because of their suffering, and there may be some truth to that. But I believe that the real reason for their strong commitment to their faith is some basic principles they live by, and that has become such a normal part of their lifestyles that no circumstance, good or bad, could convince them to change.

SIMPLICITY IN FAITH

Arthur is a Karen man whom I have known for many years. He is married to Clasper, and together they have cared for unaccompanied minors in a refugee camp in Thailand over several decades.

"My faith in God is very simple," says Arthur. "At Bible school, we studied theology and philosophy, but I always thought that the main thing is to keep our hearts clean and God will do the rest." He continues: "I have had several opportunities to go to a country in the West. I guess it would be a good opportunity, but even all the privileges in the West are useless unless they are useful. In my opinion, character is the most important thing." What Arthur says about his faith illustrates a key to the Karen people's faith: It is simple.

Many Karen do not own a Bible. Some own just part of the Bible, like the book of John. A large number of Karen people are illiterate, so even if they had access to the Bible, they would not be able to read it. There are some Bible schools, but only a lucky few are able to participate. Even the ones who have attended Bible schools cannot brag that the teaching they have received has been world class. And yet, the faith of the Karen is strong and vibrant.

They have accepted the simple truth of the gospel, and live with that truth as a compass for their lives. In our culture, we are gluttons for theology and many of us have managed to complicate our faith so much that we are no longer able to keep the simple truths as our main focus.

When one's main goal is survival, and most of one's time is spent doing exactly that, there is no time or energy left to ponder complicated issues that may not make a change in one's life. It is important not to mistake simplicity of faith with ignorance or low intelligence. That is a misconception that must not be communicated. A good example of high intelligence yet simple faith is one of the greatest leaders the Karen ever had, Saw Ba U Gyi.

Saw Ba U Gyi was the first Prime Minister of the Karen. He was elected in 1949, but in 1950 he was assassinated by the Burmese. Saw Ba U Gyi is revered by the Karen as the father of their struggle. His daughter says about his faith:

> He believed in God and worshipped him. He believed in doing unto others as you would others do unto you. The Christian faith and its way of living influenced his outlook and actions, as it does all Karen Christians. Christianity was his foundation. His education as a barrister was built on that foundation. Those two factors, coupled with his character made him the leader that he was. (Rogers, 2004:100)

It is not likely that Søren Kierkegaard had the Karen in mind when he exclaimed: "Oh, blessed simplicity, that seizes swiftly what cleverness, tired out in the service of vanity, may grasp, but slowly",[1] but it does describe them well.

SIMPLE LIFESTYLE

Our lives in the West are starting to look more and more like a constant race to get more stuff. Stuff promises happiness but, sadly, delivers headaches, divorces, depression, class differences, violence, and more besides. Richard Foster describes it well:

> We dash here and there, desperately trying to fulfill the many obligations that press upon us. We jerk back and forth between

---

[1] Kierkegaard, Søren. 1938. *Purity of Heart Is to Will One Thing*. Retrieved March 28, 2017 (http://www.naturalthinker.net/trl/texts/Kierkegaard,Soren/PurityofHeart/showchapter4.html).

commitments and family responsibilities. While we are busy responding to the needs of child and spouse, we feel guilty about neglecting the demands of work. If anyone needs simplification of life, we do. (1981:77)

This is why, according to *Introduction to Spiritual Disciplines*:

The constant sound we are bombarded with makes focusing on God and hearing his whispers in our souls much more of a daunting task. The Psalmist expressed his need for all of us when he wrote: 'Be still and know that I am God.' (Ps. 46:10)

A simple lifestyle is key to a healthy spiritual life. It seems that the more stuff we have, the harder it is to focus on God and the values that really matter. The Karen are used to having very little. This, I believe, is one of the keys to their strong commitment to their faith, and how easy it seems to be for them to practise spiritual disciplines.

In *Introduction to Spiritual Disciplines*, the author suggests that "a simple lifestyle involves choosing to live life with fewer material possessions and fewer scheduled demands". This would be true for us, but the Karen have not chosen the simple lifestyle. They have been born into it. It is a result of an unfair distribution of goods. It is also a result of a marketing economy not yet arriving with full force.

One often hears the Karen sing. When they are alone or together, they sing. I have asked myself when I last heard my neighbour sing, or when I sang myself, for that matter. The Karen's daily tasks are conducted without rush and often together with others. There is tobacco to smoke, betel nut to chew and the ingredients for a meal about to be prepared. The vegetables will be washed in a bucket of water that was just carried inside. Meat, herbs and vegetables are chopped on a slab of wood or ground in a mortar, and then prepared over the fire on the floor. Many hands join to make the meal, and those who do not have a job are content to sit and watch. The conversation comes easily. So does laughter. Their homes are not full of gadgets but it appears full of contentment and peace.

Most of the Karen I have met can pack up their belongings in a basket and carry them on their backs. Poverty ought not to be glorified, and I am not trying to do that. But I also see that the poor have something that I find very attractive: an uncluttered life. It seems that in this simple life, one more easily finds God. There is space for him. They have the time and the peace of mind to listen to him. This is a big difference between them and us.

THANKFULNESS

Foster says: "One of the most profound effects of inward simplicity is the rise of an amazing spirit of contentment" (1981:87).

Some years ago, I was in a refugee camp. All around me was poverty, and sick children and adults longing for their homes. Every person in the camp was there because their villages had been attacked and they had been forced to flee. Since they were in an official refugee camp, they all received food rations. But what they owned was just the bare minimum.

Walking through the camp, I heard worship. I asked my guide if there was a church service. It was Tuesday, so that was an uncommon time for a service. My guide replied: "Yes, one family is conducting a thanksgiving service." It surprised me. What could they be thankful for? Their lives were a study in suffering and misery. "Oh, there is a lot to be thankful for," replied my guide. "They are thankful to be alive. They are thankful they had food to eat today. They are thankful the camp hasn't been attacked. It is important to give God thanks for all the good things He has given us."

My own reaction to this episode was embarrassment. It was my habit to focus on what I *did not* have, not on what I *did* have. Compared to the refugees I visited, I was a multimillionaire. Yet, they were more thankful than I was. It may look like such a simple thing, but I believe that an attitude of thankfulness is essential in order to experience closeness to God. The Karen have understood this, and make sure to arrange times during the year where they remember God's goodness and what they are thankful for. "Godliness with contentment is great gain," said Paul (1 Tim. 6:6).

CHURCH AND COMMUNITY

The church in a Christian village is often the first building to be destroyed when soldiers attack. This is not surprising. The army understands the importance a building like this has in a small community.

The church is also one of the first structures to be rebuilt in a village when the villagers return after the attacks. It is the glue that holds the community together. It is the symbol of no surrender. It is what gives hope when hope is almost gone.

Although having a building to worship in is important for the Karen, the story in the beginning illustrates that it is the community that matters the most, not the physical structure. To some, it may seem rigid to be so uptight about worship times, especially during a time of crisis. Why have a church service in the jungle (or in the village) when there are so many other pressing issues one needs to tend to? When villages were attacked and thousands had fled, Partners[2] would get two requests. One was for emergency supplies such as food, tarps and medicine. The second request was for hymnals.

We were criticised by many for spending money on hymnals when what people needed was more food. What one needs to understand is the importance of something stable and safe, when all around is chaos. The Karen have understood something psychologists talk about, and that is the significance of routine during times of crisis and trauma.

For the Karen Christians, belonging to a church gives meaning. It gives them something to live for. For refugees and IDPs, church activities may be a way to stay sane in a world where there is not much else to live for. Their homes and farms are gone. In a refugee camp working is illegal, so days are spent idly waiting for something they doubt will ever happen. An IDP also has to sit still waiting for the soldiers to leave so that it is safe to return home again. Having church activities makes one feel useful. One can also not underestimate the importance of solitude and prayer, where they can seek the face of God for encouragement, comfort, and guidance.

---

[2] Partners Relief and Development, http://www.partners.ngo.

For the Karen, the church is the only place they ever get to hear the Word of God. Since many are illiterate, and many more do not own a Bible, hearing a sermon on Sunday and other days means a lot to their personal faith. Indeed, it is no wonder why the army has been so eager to destroy churches. It is the heart of many communities.

Worship and Prayer

As previously mentioned, the Karen sing a lot. An important part of their culture is singing together. One never has to walk far to hear a group of Karen singing in harmony. Very often, the songs sung are old and well-loved hymns. The church services may seem old-fashioned and stiff to many, with long liturgies and non-charismatic sermons. The songs are mostly songs that have been sung for decades, if not centuries.

It is not until one gets to know the Karen and how dear the songs are to them that one can appreciate the importance of choirs and endless song practices fully. The music binds them together as a community. The songs define their culture and their faith. It is their history. And ultimately, the words they sing remind them of their God.

Prayer is a mystery, and even more so when watching oppressed people pray and not getting the desired answer. Stassen and Gushee's statement rings true: "It is easy to conclude that Jesus rather cruelly fostered a pious illusion when he promised that all your prayers will be answered with good things, when obviously they are not" (2003:458). But the Karen still pray. God is a part of every decision they make and their lives are committed to Him on a constant basis. They have asked for deliverance for many decades.

Still, they are not free. "Our hope is in heaven," they smile confidently. "We may never get our freedom here on earth, but our hope is heaven." Again, their simple answer is a difficult one. In the West, we want everything instantly. We want fast internet. We want fast cars. We want fast food and fast weight loss. The idea of waiting is not appealing to us and this is reflected in the way we see prayer as well. For the Karen, it is different. Their lives are spent waiting.

I have sat with Karen people on the side of the road waiting for a ride for hours. Nobody knew when a car would show up, and the only one who seemed to care was me. To them, waiting is a part of life. I think that is why prayer for them is closer to what real prayer is: conversations with God without expecting an instant answer.

"But they that wait upon the Lord shall renew their strength; they shall mount up with wings as eagles; they shall run, and not be weary; and they shall walk, and not faint" (Isa. 40:31; KJV).

FORGIVENESS

When you think you have heard the worst stories there are, they will tell you one that is even worse. The suffering of the Karen is long and brutal. They all have stories of losses, big and small. For 50 years they were on the run. They never knew when the next attack would come. I have spent hours with the victims of the war, hearing their stories, and documenting them. The questions I have often asked are: Do you hate the Burmese? Does all the suffering make you doubt God?

There are, of course, many who hate the Burmese and who want revenge. Anything else would be strange. But surprisingly often I will hear this: "We cannot hate them. If we don't forgive, we will become like them." Others will say: "The soldiers don't know what they are doing. They are just following orders. We cannot hate them." One of the Karen's most beloved leaders, Mary On, said this: "We don't hate the Burmans, we hate the system, a system which kills, plunders, loots and rapes."

Another pastor, who does not want his name published, said: "I didn't want to love the Burmans, but the Bible tells me to. And many soldiers are innocent—they are simply under orders—and so we try to love the people who need love." Once he sent a letter to the Burmese soldiers. Among other things, he wrote: "Friends, I know your situation. I love you. Maybe now you feel alone. Maybe now you want to go home. Don't be anxious or afraid, because God loves you." He concluded with: "We pray for your government, for wisdom for your government, for peace of mind and love and hope for your leaders."

Our dear friend, a Karen widow whose husband had been killed and who was living in a refugee camp with two young children, illustrated forgiveness in a very tangible way. When a Burma soldier entered the refugee camp where she was living, all the people there looked at him as the hated enemy. He embodied why they were prisoners, unable to go back to their homes. He was the image of the man who had raped or killed their loved ones. He was the tormentor. He did, however, say he was a deserter. Our friend Rose was the only one who believed him, and who decided to give him a chance. She took him in, gave him a job at her orphanage, and shared the love and forgiveness of Jesus with him. The result was a changed man.

Forgiveness is often overlooked. Perhaps it is not considered a spiritual discipline. For the Karen, it is. Without forgiving the ones who have hurt them so much, for such a long time, they cannot draw close to God. The Bible is full of verses encouraging forgiveness; Jesus' example is clear. "Bear with each other and forgive one another if any of you has a grievance against someone. Forgive as the Lord forgave you" (Col. 3:13). To date, I have only heard one kind of answer to my question about doubting God's goodness in the midst of all the suffering: "Don't make us doubt God. He didn't make this suffering happen. Man did. If you take our hope in God, away we have nothing." The responses have been so adamant and clear that I understand that this is very important for my friends.

Christian Godden asked Saw Joshua the same question as I have asked: "Saw Joshua, when asked if he felt bitter, laughed: 'How could we ever be bitter to the Lord after all he has done for us? No, we are thankful for his goodness and pray that we will learn whatever lessons he has for us in this present situation'" (1996:282).

HOSPITALITY

One cannot write about the Karen without mentioning their hospitality and generosity. Even when they are desperately poor, they will always share whatever they have with a guest. "A guest could be Jesus," they explain. I cannot help but wonder if they know that what they are saying is straight from Jesus' mouth—"I was a stranger, and you invited me in" (Matt. 25:35). The Karen do not just share their food with any guest who comes to their houses. Their tradition is also to let the guest eat first, and whatever he or she does not eat the hosts get to eat. My husband shares the story of arriving late at night in a poor Karen village. The villagers had no food left for themselves or for the guests that had arrived. Not knowing what else to do, one of the villagers went and killed one of the dogs in the village, which they cooked and served the guests.

The Karen have understood the importance of hospitality better than we have in our part of the world. The Bible is full of verses admonishing us to be hospitable (see Acts 2:44–45; Acts 28:7; Titus 1:8 and 1 Tim. 3:2, just to mention a few). Perhaps without knowing it, they are in the same room as Jesus. It is a lesson that ought to be learned by the leaders in our own rich countries. It seems that the "love of strangers" (translation of the word "hospitality") gets weaker as we get richer. Forgotten is the admonition from Leviticus 19:33–34: "When an alien lives with you in your land, do not mistreat him. The alien living with you must be treated as one of your native-born. Love him as yourself, for you were aliens in Egypt."

The poor and the oppressed may be closer to the heart of God for this reason: They treat the visitor, the stranger, the alien, as if he or she was Jesus.

CONCLUSION

When studying an oppressed people group like the Karen, it is easy to idealise them and their culture, and to be blind to the negative aspects of their culture and lifestyle. I do not want to come across as gullible and naïve. Just as there are exceptions to every other rule, there are exceptions to the rules of Karen Christianity as well. Not all Karen are forgiving and selfless. Not all Karen are content. Not all Karen Christians are thankful all the time. I am aware of that.

What I have tried to write here are examples of things I have seen in their culture that has impressed me and that have explained how they have been able to keep their faith in the midst of suffering and poverty. It is my constant prayer that they will experience freedom and liberty, and that they will have enough food to eat and schools for their children to attend. I am not opposed to development. What I do hope, however, is that development will not take them away from the things that really matter. Like Arthur said to me when he considered moving to a Western country: "It is useless if it is not useful," and, "Some people are never content." He was a contented man who saw the dangers of moving to a nation where contentment and simplicity have become foreign expressions with unknown meaning for many.

What does spirituality mean to me personally and to our organisation?

The faith of the Karen has already changed me personally forever. I often tell people that from the Karen I have learned more about what it means to be a true follower of Jesus than I could have learned at any seminary, or under any world-famous preacher.

For us as an organisation,[3] it has also meant a lot to work with a people group who are so dedicated to values that align with the values of the Bible. We may be able to teach them sustainable development and give emergency relief when needed. We can treat their sick and start microcredit schemes. But when it comes to their faith and commitment to God and their people, it is *they* who teach us. We can supplement by buying hymnals and giving sponsorships for Bible schools. We can share at Bible studies and church services. But when we do, it is always as learners and with an attitude that says: We can share with you what we have, but you must understand that it is just as important for us to learn from you.

Pastor Simon, a Karen pastor who has a remarkable story of endurance and commitment to his people, says this:

---

[3] Partners Relief and Development

They call us displaced people,
But praise God; we are not misplaced.
They say they see no hope for our future,
But praise God; our future is as bright as the promises of God.
They say they see the life of our people is a misery,
But praise God; our life is a mystery.
For what they say is what they see, and what they see is temporal.
But ours is eternal.
All because we put ourselves
In the hands of the God we trust.

May we all have an outlook on life like Pastor Simon. He has suffered much, and been denied what we would consider basic rights. Still, he is able to praise God.

REFERENCES

Authentic Discipleship. 2011. "Introduction to Spiritual Disciplines." Retrieved June 2015 (http://www.authenticdiscipleship.org/pdfs/2-spiritual-formation/Spiritual%20Disciplines/SF%201.0%20Introduction%20to%20the%20Spiritual%20Disciples.pdf).

Foster, Richard. 1981. *Freedom of Simplicity*. New York, NY: HarperCollins.

Godden, Christian. 1996. *Three Pagodas: A Journey Down the Thai-Burmese Border*. Halesworth, UK: Jungle Books.

Greenman, Jeffrey P. 2010. "Spiritual Formation in Theological Perspective." Pp. 23–35 in *Life in the Spirit: Spiritual Formation in Theological Perspective*, edited by Jeffrey P. Greenman and George Kalantzis. Downers Grove, IL: InterVarsity Press.

Marshall, Harry Ignatius. 1922. *The Karen People of Burma*. Columbus, OH: The University.

Neiman, Amy, Eunice Soh, and Parisa Sutan. (2008). "Karen Cultural Profile." *Ethnomed*. Retrieved June 2015 (https://ethnomed.org/culture/karen/karen-cultural-profile).

Richardson, Don. 1980. *Eternity in their Hearts*. Ventura, CA: Regal Books.

Rogers, Benedict. 2004. *A Land without Evil*. Oxford, UK: Monarch Books.

Smeaton, Donald Mackenzie. 1920. *The Loyal Karens of Burma*. London: K. Paul, Trench, Trubner & Co.

Stassen, Glen H. and David P. Gushee. 2003. *Kingdom Ethics: Following Jesus in Contemporary Context*. Downers Grove, IL: InterVarsity Press.

EASTERN
COLLEGE AUSTRALIA
Be challenged. Be change.

Eastern College Australia is a registered Higher Education Provider that provides
teaching, training and research from a Christian worldview. It contributes to
the Church and human flourishing through the lives of its graduates. Eastern
is committed to providing high quality, government-accredited awards from
Certificate to Masters, currently focusing on three major areas of study: Education,
Theology, Arts & Social Sciences.

Melbourne School of Theology is a non-denominational Bible college, based in the
outer eastern suburbs of Melbourne. Since 1920, MST has been passionate about
training those with a heart for ministry and mission with a solid Biblical grounding
in God's Word. MST also offers practical experience in ministry, working closely
with local churches and mission and para-church organisations.

GRACEWORKS

Graceworks is a publishing and training consultancy based in Singapore, with
a passion to promote spiritual friendship in church and society and see lives
transformed through books that present truth for life.
You can find more of our books at our online store www.graceworks.com.sg

www.ingramcontent.com/pod-product-compliance
Lightning Source LLC
Chambersburg PA
CBHW071740120626
46550CB00002B/591